cocoon house

cocoon house

LIGHT IN SUSTAINABLE ARCHITECTURE AND DESIGN

 Artifice

Undertaken in a mode of research by design, this monograph seeks to offer a productive response to the opportunities and shortcomings of current theories, techniques and practices of environmental design in architecture, with specific reference to solar design.

Designers today face increasing environmental and market pressures, which they can counter by producing and creating the conditions for affective experiences. Exploring the layers of environmental design will help us to understand the relations between nature, technology and perception. Architects and designers must begin to integrate these important environmental strategies and emerging technologies into their work, given the current environmental crisis we are living in.

Foreword
DAVID LEATHERBARROW

Light was the theme of Louis Kahn's proposal for a more humane and situated modern architecture. No less thoughtful, but more wide-eyed in its vision of architecture and its environment (the one we know is in crisis), Nina Edwards Anker's written and built work marshals contributions from historians, philosophers, environmentalists and artists to disclose the reality and richness of affective experience, as it is sustained by furnishings, architectural elements and entire buildings. Cloud-white walls, stone-gray shadows and skin-tan slabs cool and warm settings that elegantly and insistently refuse the categorical distinction between works of art and nature, architecture's in- and out-side. The integrative light that brightens these pages emerges from things just as much as it envelopes them, thanks to really smart design.

David Leatherbarrow, Professor at the University of Pennsylvania, is a writer, thinker and teacher concerned with the theory and practice of architecture.

Contents

Introduction   EMBODIED SUNLIGHT   **11**

Chapter One   THE AFFECTIVE SENSE
OF SOLAR THINGS

15   Why Environmental Aesthetics?
16   Affect—the Cognitive Position
23   The Scientific
25   The Synaesthetic
31   The Situational
32   Time, Temperature, Scale and Material
42   The Felt Sense

Chapter Two   THINGS

45   Thingness
48   Biophilia

BIOPHILIC LIGHTING
AND FURNITURE

50   Algae Lamp
50   Beanie Sofa
51   Knotty Set
51   Cantilever Table
51   Crystallised Set
55   Cape Chair
55   Outdoor Twist Sofa
56   Vanity Table
56   Bird Bed and Chair

SOLAR THINGS

57   Latitude Lamp
61   Sun Calendar
64   Solar Chandelier
65   Solar Lounger

Chapter Three   ARCHITECTURE

67   Introduction
135   Cocoon House
152   Concluding Thoughts

Chapter Four   CONCLUSIONS

157   Sensing Solar Cells
162   Drawings

Bibliography   **168**
Biographical Note   **172**
Acknowledgements   **173**
Credits   **175**

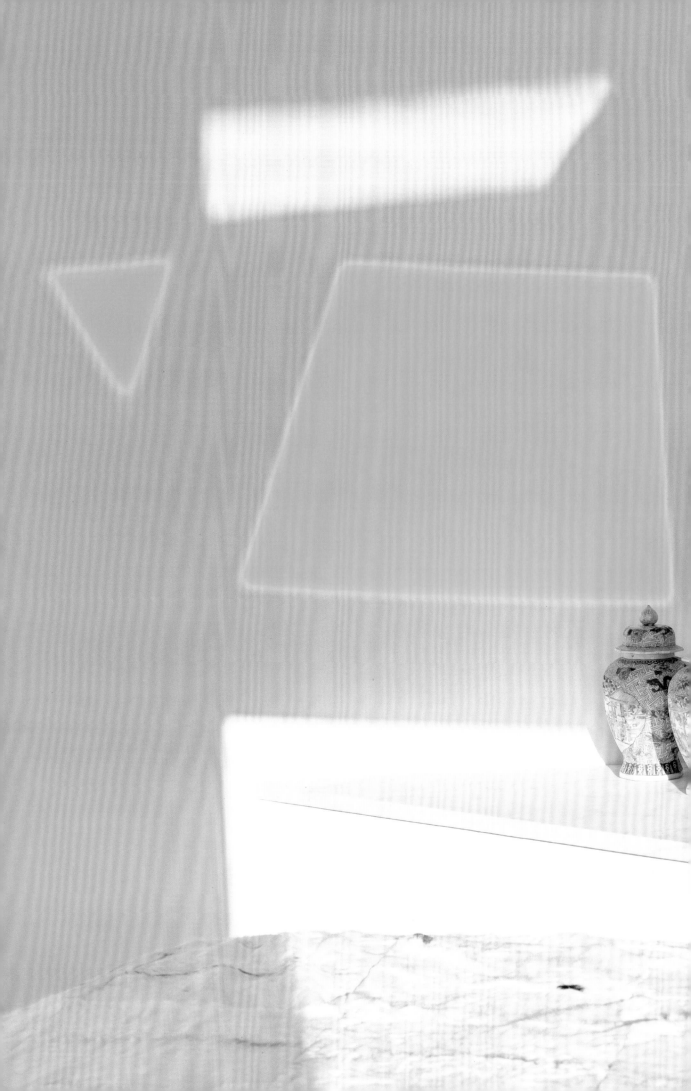

Introduction
EMBODIED SUNLIGHT

1 The view from above has been discussed by theorists such as Jeanne Haffner, *The View from Above—The Science of Social Space*, Cambridge, MA: MIT Press, 2013. See also Nina Edwards Anker and Peder Anker, "Viewing the Earth from Without or from Within", *New Geographies* 4, Cambridge, MA: Harvard Graduate School of Design, 2011.

2 Husserl, Edmund, "Foundational Investigations of the Phenomenological Origin of the Spatiality of Nature: The Originary Ark, the Earth, Does Not Move," in *Husserl at the Limits of Phenomenology*, Leonard Lawlor with Bettina Bergo, eds, Fred Kersten, trans, Leonard Lawlor rev, Evanston, IL: Northwestern University, 2002, pp 117–131, quote p 118.

3 Sarkis, Hashim, "New Geographies: Notes on an Emerging Aesthetics", *New Geographies* 0, Cambridge, MA, Harvard Graduate School of Design publication, 2008, pp 98–109, quote p 101.

4 Patočka, Jan, *Body, Community, Language, World*, James Dodd, ed, Erazim Kohák, trans, Chicago and La Salle, IL: Open Court, 1998, p xvii.

5 Anker and Anker, "Viewing the Earth from Without or from Within", p 89.

The drive towards energy-saving technologies poses new challenges to the architectural and design community. One of these is to ensure that solutions to current problems do not come at the expense of the emotional and social needs of their human audiences.[1] People are unlikely to incorporate environmental architecture and design into their everyday lives if they do not find them attractive.

Can solar design bring humans and the planet closer together? If so, how? More specifically, how can solar architecture embody sunlight in a way that is *affective*? This study attempts to answer these questions by looking beyond the limited technical function of environmental technologies used in projects such as Cocoon.

Solar design and architecture partake of a complex energy system in which commercial forces play a pivotal role. Though the solar industry aims first and foremost to generate energy, it is also prey to market pressures and the demands of corporate capitalism. As a result, architects and designers who work with renewable energy systems tend to devise solutions that are cost-driven and technologically efficient. The design profession is also confronted by additional pressures, such as payback time and the push for spectacular effects made possible by digital technologies.

The problem is that when solar designs are financially and technologically determined from *without*, by outside forces, they can detract from the sun's influence on human experience from *within*. To counter such a tendency, this book proposes that design conform to Edmund Husserl's horizontal perspective: "The Earth is a spherical body, certainly not perceivable in its wholeness all at once and by one person; rather, it is perceived in a primordial synthesis as a unity of mutually connected single experiences."[2] According to this view, the Earth resists external mapping and planning of its surface and artefacts, asserting instead a "condition of flux",[3] in accordance with a concept of the human body that Jan Patočka calls a "personal situatedness" among things: "The dynamic I am cannot be fully grasped from a distance, as a movement we can observe from the outside, but must rather be grasped from within, as a situation always 'mine'."[4]

While the view from outside is aerial and zooms down towards the local, the one from inside originates in the human and extends out towards the horizon.[5] Therefore, eco-ethical and financial incentives alone, which are often

6   The field of Research by Design in this case is situated at the Architecture Department of the Oslo School of Design, where this book was researched and where the term was heavily debated during faculty meetings. While some took the more empirical, evidence-based approach to the field, others adopted an intuitive approach based in phenomenological philosophy that engaged the agency of the designer or architect.

7   The researchers at the Biomimetic Robotics Lab at the Massachusetts Institute of Technology (MIT), for instance, take inspiration from biology and underemphasise the role of the designer in their transfer of knowledge from biology to design. Biomimetics.mit.edu, accessed 29 January 2015.

8   "[Affects] are both superficial and immersive, two features that correspond especially well to the characteristics of present-day ornament." Antoine Picon, "Reinventing the Meaning of Ornament" (Chap 4), in *Ornament—The Politics of Architecture and Subjectivity*, Sussex, UK: Wiley, 2013, pp 129–155.

9   Since this book focuses on the experience from within, rather than the view from without, the sense of sight is not included as a factor influencing solar design, unless it leads to and incorporates the other senses.

imposed from without, cannot encourage the adoption of environmental technologies because they do not take the full human into account. This is why the solar industry attracts minimal attention from consumers, architects and designers. When transferring knowledge from science, some practitioners of Research by Design tend not to emphasise the role of the designer.[6] By contrast, this book focuses on artistic agency and,[7] drawing on the theory of French philosopher Maurice Merleau-Ponty, proposes a way of designing with environmental technologies that stimulates mind and body together.

The discussion presented here revolves around the question of *affect*. However, affect theory is not yet a clearly defined field and, when applied to architectural design, it is usually done only in a superficial way. As historian of architecture and technology Antoine Picon points out, the digitally generated 'affective' ornamental surfaces of much contemporary architecture offer a shallow sensual experience, but fail to stimulate the mind.[8] However, the mediation of sunlight through solar cells could promote multi-sensory experiences while also heightening our awareness of design and architectural space in both a physiological and cerebral way. Such a mind-body connection would entail a shift in our understanding of sunlight, but if we are made to feel and see the rhythms of light and shadow through the filter of solar architecture, we might become more conscious of sunlight as a powerful natural process.

If solar architecture and design can stimulate the senses by modulating heat and light, they can also engage the faculties of memory and awareness of time to mediate between nature and technology, in ways that reveal, yet transcend, the physiological realm. In such cases, architecture or design can shape users' perception so they experience sunlight in 'green' architecture and design in a new manner. Cocoon House provides the context in which this transformation may occur.

This shift towards affect and away from the problematic way in which people often approach sustainable design is inspired by the philosophy of Merleau-Ponty and his definition of the scientific, the synaesthetic and the situational. As the Cocoon House is powered by solar cells, discussion centres on the capacity of architecture to activate processes that relate to the sun—namely, time, temperature, scale and material.

What makes an encounter between an artefact of technological design and a human an affective one? Our senses of time, temperature, scale and material are particularly relevant to solar design: the sun helps us tell time, emits heat and operates at multiple scales, from the molecular to the cosmic (the sense of sight is omitted here as a criterion to avoid an overly ocular-centric approach to design[9]). Our sense of time can be awoken by seeing shadows cast in dynamic patterns, which can be electrically engineered by LED bulbs to synchronise with solar rhythms (one of the models used here automatically replays the passage of the sun at dusk). Solar design can sharpen our sense of temperature through

10 Kronenburg, Robert, *Spirit of the Machine—Technology as an Inspiration in Architectural Design*, UK: Wiley-Academy, 2001, p 62.

11 Dean Hawkes, Hal Foster, Kenneth Frampton, Hashim Sarkis, Olafur Eliasson, Sheila Kennedy, etc.

12 Brian Massumi, Antoine Picon, Hélène Frichot, Sylvia Lavin and others.

thermal stimulation, and our sense of scale by connecting humans with local contexts. It can also heighten our sense of material by combining glossy new solar panels with contrasting materials, such as those that acquire a glossy patina over time (eg, rust), assume a classical form (eg, the cube or sphere), or are deemed organic or 'primal' (eg, wood or stone).[10]

Solar design should thus aim to be more engaging and enduring—in short, to be more affective. By using photovoltaic material to collect the power of the sun, and by channelling daylight into interior and exterior spaces, solar design can enrich sensory and cognitive awareness, as well as facilitate connectivity between humans and the planet.

A host of architects and designers have written about environmental technologies in architecture and design,[11] and many scholars have discussed the concept of affect in architecture.[12] By focusing on a specific example, this book aims to contribute to this broader discussion. Given the current environmental crisis, we can no longer afford to ignore the opportunities presented by solar architecture and design, or this potentially fertile field will fail to flourish.

Chapter One
THE AFFECTIVE SENSE OF SOLAR THINGS

1 Lovins, Amory and Robert Bradley, Jr, "Energy Strategy: The Road not Taken", *Foreign Affairs Journal*, 1976; "Remembering the Birth of Conservatism, Part II: Amory Lovins' "Soft Energy Path", 3 May 2011, mastersource.org, accessed 20 December 2013.

2 "Urban Omnibus, Multitasking Infrastructures: A Conversation with Sheila Kennedy and Veit Kugel", 2013, urbanomnibus.net, accessed 11 March 2014.

3 Harries, Karsten, "What Need is There for an Environmental Aesthetics?", *The Nordic Journal of Aesthetics*, 40–41, 2010–2011, pp 21, 801.

In 1976, Amory Lovins coined the term 'soft energy paths' to describe power generated by a public activity rather than by a centralised engineering project.[1] As opposed to 'hard' power fuelled by oil, gas, coal or uranium, the soft energy paths in his designs were meant to exemplify a form of decentralised, renewable technology that conserves energy. American architect Sheila Kennedy later came up with the term 'soft infrastructure' to describe designs that combine several sources of energy working together to promote resilience and adaptability.[2] This project aims to take Kennedy and Lovins' definition of soft, rather than conventional hard, infrastructural systems as its model, by adopting materials that interact with their environments and social settings.

Why Environmental Aesthetics?

If we are to alleviate global warming at a more rapid pace, we need to ask ourselves the right questions. To effect radical change, we first need to modify our attitude to solar energy. The key question is not how sustainable architecture and design can improve the environment, but how they can initiate a dialogue between humans and the planet. This book therefore addresses the humanisation of our planet by examining how the building techniques and technologies of solar architecture and design can influence human perception, and discusses a series of works that reduce global/planetary scale to that of the human being.

In his article "What Need is there for an Environmental Aesthetics?", German philosopher Karsten Harries calls for a dialogue between humans and the planet that will search for new ways of relating to the environment through design, and thus address society's lack of environmental awareness:

> To change the way we relate to the environment we need more than just cold reason [....] What is required is a change of heart. But how do hearts change? [....] An environmental aesthetics, I have here suggested, is needed to help pry open a window or door in the architecture that reason, which rightly rules over our science and technology, has built us; a window to a dimension of our experience and of reality that transcends the reach of such reason.[3]

"We find certain things fascinating
because they exert a pull on us through
what philosophers call 'affect'."

In Harries' view, global warming cannot, then, be addressed by reason alone, and conventional scientific methods used to research climate change are limited, as proven by our lack of progress in addressing greenhouse gas emissions thus far. It will take more than science and technology to achieve the required degree of change since peoples' decisions are not motivated by reason or ethical imperatives alone. Harries goes on to ask what an "environmental aesthetics" might look like, suggesting that it might involve "an aesthetics so fundamentally transformed that we may well wonder whether aesthetics remains an appropriate name".[4]

As stated in the Introduction, society tends to see global environmental technologies 'from without' in terms of energy and price efficiencies, while failing to recognise the perspective 'from within'. Most solar companies sell their products as purely technological items and, as a result, many architects and designers choose not to include them in their designs. As Harries suggests, what is needed is a type of design that addresses the global warming crisis in a more transformative and comprehensive manner.

Affect—the Cognitive Position

Introduced here is the notion of *affect*, which can respond to Harries' call for a "change of heart", as it compels us to revisit such basic concepts as the opposition between emotion and reason. Some of the most innovative and productive theoretical and epistemological trends of the past three decades have drawn on affect and demonstrated its centrality to everyday life. All the same, there is no consensus on what exactly it is. This volume sets out to contribute to that debate,[5] and to demonstrate how the notion of affect may be applied to sustainable design.

We find certain things fascinating because they exert a pull on us through what philosophers call 'affect'. Today, this term is often applied to the milieu of design. The concept itself, however, dates back to Aristotle, and the English term for it derives from the Latin noun *affectus*. On its initial introduction to the English language in the 1300s, the word was used to describe powerful emotions, such as joy, sorrow or love. In the seventeenth century, Dutch philosopher Baruch Spinoza defined affect as a state of mind and body related to, but different from, emotions, in that it was more transformative in nature. In the twentieth century, French philosopher Gilles Deleuze modified the meaning of the term to denote a change in intensity that involves the body and its surrounding space and time. From Deleuze's perspective, affects are blocks of space-time, which, unlike personal emotions, are not connected to a subject's mind, but rather to a more

4 Harries, "What Need Is There for Environmental Aesthetics?", p 21.

5 I attempt to contribute to the fields of cultural studies and affect theory by narrowing in on a single material, the photovoltaic panel, in order to address a problem noted by cultural theorist Lawrence Grossberg, that "affect covers too much ground". Lawrence Grossberg, "Affect's Future", *The Affect Theory Reader,* Melissa Gregg and Gregory J Seigworth, eds, Durham, NC, and London, UK: Duke University Press, 2010, p 314.

6 Deleuze, Gilles and Felix Guattari, *A Thousand Plateaus—Capitalism and Schizophrenia*, Minneapolis, MN, London, UK: University of Minnesota Press, 1987, p xvi.

7 Rawsthorn, Alice, "Defining the Emotional Cause of 'Affect'—Farshid Moussavi's 'Architecture and Affects' installation at the Venice Architecture Biennale", *The New York Times*, Art & Design, 2 Dec 2012, accessed 1 June 2015.

8 Lam, William C, *Perception and Lighting as Formgivers in Architecture*, Christopher Hugh Ripman, ed, New York, NY, St. Louis, MO, San Francisco, CA: McGraw Hill, 1977, p 8.

9 A stimulus is "anything which excites a sensory receptor, causing or regarded as causing a response or sensation", Lam, *Perception and Lighting*, p 9.

10 Schachter, Stanley, and Jerome Singer, "Cognitive, Social, and Physiological Determinants of Emotional State", *Psychological Review*, vol 69, no 5, 1962.

11 Tomkins, Silvan, *Affect Imagery Consciousness: Volume I, The Positive Affects*, London, UK: Tavistock, 1962.

12 When Tomkins' views began garnering more support in the 1980s, American psychologist Richard S Lazarus, renowned for his cognitive-mediational theory of emotion, took issue with those who claimed that affect and cognition were separate systems. In 1994, following Lazarus' lead, American psychologist Alan J Fridlund attacked the empirical and theoretical claims underlying the 'anti-cognitive' model. Similarly, American philosopher and psychologist Eugene T Gendlin has continued to oppose the anti-cognitive paradigm and to argue for the importance of the interaction between ideas and directly felt experience, as he does in *Focusing* (New York: Bantam Books, 2007), a work much indebted to Maurice Merleau-Ponty.

generalised superficial state.[6] Now, in the twenty-first century, the Deleuzian meaning of the term is common in architectural discourse.

The language used to describe the way in which design impacts the senses is often imprecise. Some designers and design theorists view the confusing tangle of sensations provoked by design as transformations in atmosphere, spirit, mood or tone. The discussion of the term presented here aims to clarify and identify the ways in which design influences people, and how its power to do so can be put to intelligent use. Discussing the way in which the classic Thonet chair generates affect, for example, British design critic and author Alice Rawsthorn discusses the importance of understanding its cause and nature:

> Back in 1859, the first No. 14s promised to combine the reliability of industrial production with the emotional warmth of wood. Over 150 years later, we still find that combination reassuring, while sensing that there is something unexpected about it, bold even. Each of us will interpret the affects of Thonet's chair slightly differently, but the impression they produce is very powerful, which is why understanding that sensation is not just important to designers but to us too.[7]

Rather than involving merely the reception of sensations—the immediate result of the stimulation of the sense organs—*perception* ensues from a combination of incoming sensations, contextual information and past experience which, together, allow us to recognise and assign meaning to the objects or events from which stimuli arise. William Lam, a pioneer of architectural lighting design, defines perception as "a meaningful impression obtained through the senses and apprehended by the mind".[8] *Affect* (the noun), on the other hand, is a dimension of behaviour, experienced at the same time as perception, performance and thought. The Thonet chair is affective because it activates a cognitive evaluation and/or emotional response,[9] which derives from multiple factors, including the emotional impact of its material and its associations with 'warmth', along with its sense of comfort and aesthetic charm.

American social psychologists Stanley Schachter and Jerome E Singer claim that affect has two dimensions: physiological arousal and a cognitive label. In their study of 1962,[10] they tested how people rely on cues in their environment to explain physiological changes, and used the results to confirm their hypothesis that affect and cognition are indissociable. That same year saw the rise of a rival approach related to the work of American psychologist Silvan Tomkins,[11] who insisted that affect and cognition were two separate systems. Although Schachter-Singer's theory initially prevailed, the anticognitive one proposed by Tomkins gradually displaced it to become the mainstream model in the 1990s, accepted by the majority of today's theorists in the humanities and social sciences.

The anticognitive paradigm has nevertheless been criticised over the years by psychoanalysts, philosophers and scientists.[12] Psychoanalysts, for example,

13 Ruth Leys lines up the ongoing debate between
two opposing sides of researchers and theorists:
"On one side are the cognitivists—appraisal
psychologists such as Richard Lazarus, social
constructionists such as Rom Harre, and many
philosophers, such as Anthony Kenny, Robert
Solomon, Peter Goldie, and Martha Nussbaum,
all of whom in the post-World War II period have
stressed the intentionality of the emotions, but are
thought to have trouble accommodating the
existence of emotions in non-human animals (or
infants before they acquire language). On the other
side are the noncognitivists, postwar psychologists
such as [Silvan] Tomkins, [Paul] Ekman, and [Carroll]
Izard, and philosophers such as [Paul E] Griffiths,
who, often influenced by Darwinian considerations
and the work of William James, have emphasized
the importance of bodily changes and subpersonal
processes in the emotions but are seen to have
difficulty explaining how emotions have meaning."
Ruth Leys, The Ascent of Affect: Genealogy and
Critique, Chicago, IL, and London, UK: The University
of Chicago Press, 2017, p 3.

14 Massumi also translated Deleuze and Guattari's
A Thousand Plateaus.

15 Highmore, Ben, "Bitter after Taste", The Affect
Theory Reader, Melissa Gregg and Gregory J
Seigworth, eds, Durham, NC, and London, UK:
Duke University Press, 2010, p 119.

16 Sandaker, Bjørn Normann, On Span and Space—
Exploring Structures in Architecture, London, UK,
and New York, NY: Routledge, 2008, pp 115–116.

17 Anthes, Emily , "How Room Designs Affect Your
Work and Mood—Brain Research Can Help Us
Craft Spaces that Relax, Inspire, Awaken, Comfort
and Heal", Scientific American, April/May/June
2009, scientificamerican.com/article/building-
around-the-mind/, accessed 5 January 2015.

have always associated affect with meaning, as they see close connections between emotion and cognition, or belief. When undergoing psychotherapy, the individual studies, evaluates and rethinks his or her values and concepts via an experiential process that serves as a basis for the fabrication of ideas.

Championing the cognitive model, the view of affect offered in the designs presented here takes Schachter-Singer's alternative route,[13] and thus runs against present-day Deleuzian scholars such as the Canadian social theorist Brian Massumi,[14] and American political theorist William Connolly, both of whom separate affect from cognition. The cognitive model insists that cognition and intention play crucial roles in the development of human behaviour, and argues that recent theoretical approaches to affect focus too narrowly on the personal sensual process of perception at the expense of shared ethical imperatives and cultural heritage. As British cultural and art historian Ben Highmore writes, "a body free of the trappings (and traps) of discourse, of culture, might not be much of a human body at all."[15] Exploring similar avenues of thought, Norwegian author and engineer Bjørn Normann Sandaker, too, discusses how the intellectual and emotional interpretation sought by the observer is necessarily integrated into aesthetic experience: "The experience we seek is one of pleasure, but not simply sensuous pleasure."[16]

Many designers of the past have also intuited that the places we inhabit and the designs that surround us have the power to affect not only our feelings and behaviours, but also our thoughts. In 2009, behavioural scientists started proving with empirical data that certain factors in the design of spaces could stimulate activities such as social interaction and creativity, and promote relaxation, focus and alertness. Indeed, some schools of architecture now offer classes in introductory neuroscience, while institutions like the Academy of Neuroscience for Architecture in San Diego encourage interdisciplinary research on the influence of different types of planned environments on the mind.[17]

The formulation of affect presented here maintains that ideas interact with directly felt experience. This study views an affective encounter as a visceral moment of perception that includes cognition, but what is of particular interest for our purpose is how the cognitive relates to the sensual and emotional in our experience of solar design. Four parameters will be used to link the cognitive, sensual and emotional together: awareness of time, temperature, scale and material. All are derived from the defining characteristics of the sun, which marks time by moving across the sky rhythmically, generates heat, and relates to the scale of the distant solar system by generating power via the material of the photovoltaic panel. These four parameters are all derived from the activity of light, which appeals above all to the sense of sight. However, vision is deliberately omitted in our discussion of affect in order to underline and bring forth other types of sensory awareness that have traditionally often been ignored, and to avoid the ocular centrism of treating vision as the primary sense relevant to design.

"Affect (the noun) (…) is a dimension of behaviour, experienced at the same time as perception, performance and thought."

The four chosen parameters outlined above also branch out to further multiple psychological and physical senses, such as those of security and touch, while at the same time triggering awareness of power generation and its eco-ethical implications. The goal is to establish a number of essential design principles that link the sensual with the cognitive, and to understand how certain abstract ideas, such as climate change, may relate to sensual reception.

Rather than aiming for essential design principles, however, contemporary architects have often embraced complexity. As Marc Treib states:

> There seems to be little question that we live in an age of complexity, perhaps undue complexity. Internet access, the interrelation of almost all the people all the time, the pressures of urbanization, natural resource depletion, increasing traffic and pollution, and our ability to be anywhere at any time electronically—all have led to a rather complex living mode indeed. Architects, heeding the call, have produced an architecture correspondingly complex.[18]

Many architects and designers also see affect as the reflection of such complexity, by creating complicated shapes and elaborate ornament that generate intensity through sensual stimulation. A notable example is London-based architect Farshid Moussavi's contribution to the 2012 Venice Architecture Biennale, entitled *Architecture and its Affects*, an installation of giant projected images of various architectural styles and structures that relied on shapes, decorative elements and methods of construction to generate multiple affects in visitors' noncognitive, sensual processes of perception. As Moussavi explains: "Whereas meanings are dependent on an individual's biographical background, affects are pre-personal intensities of built forms. They are solely the consequence of how built forms are assembled: the systems and technology used, where and for what purpose."[19]

In as much as Moussavi claims that affects are "pre-personal", one may argue that affects are also personal and have meanings. Indeed, Moussavi regards affect as a generic thing in itself,[20] an assessment that robs it of its power to convey messages. Yet the affect transmitted by a design can be intertwined with its meaning, which in turn may emanate from the affect's origins in a specific location or tradition connected to the viewer's biography. Meaning is embedded in affect because it arises in part from personal history, and in part from an awareness of shared cultural heritage. In the case of solar designs, meaning can also derive from ethical imperatives. To carry import, therefore, affect entails more than superficial sensual stimulation and must reach people on a cognitive level.

18 Treib, Marc, "Simplicity and Belief", *Quality out of Control: Standards for Measuring*, Allison Dutoit, Juliet Odgers, and Adam Sharr, eds, London, UK, and New York, NY: Routledge, 2010, p 119.

19 Saieh, Nico, "Venice Biennale 2012: Architecture and its Affects / Farshid Moussavi", *ArchDaily*, 4 Sep 2012, archdaily.com/269585/venice-biennale-2012-farshid-moussavi/, accessed 1 May 2015.

20 See description of John Lewis Department Store and Cineplex, farshidmoussavi.com, accessed 15 Jan 2015.

"Meaning is em
because it arises i
history, and in par
of shared cultura
of solar designs
derive from eth

dded in affect

art from personal

rom an awareness

eritage. In the case

neaning can also

al imperatives."

21 Cited in Christian Lotz, *From Affectivity to Subjectivity—Husserl's Phenomenology Revisited*, Hampshire, UK, and New York, NY: Palgrave Macmillan, 2007, p 143, note 29.

22 "We move toward and away from objects through how we are affected by them." Sara Ahmed, "Happy Objects", *The Affect Theory Reader*, Melissa Gregg and Gregory Seigworth, eds, Durham, NC, and London, UK: Duke University Press, 2010, p 32.

23 Ibid.

24 As American philosopher and psychologist William James put it, "Our voluntary attention is always derived; we never make an effort to attend to an object except for the sake of some interest which the effort will serve." William James, *The Principles of Psychology*, vol 1, New York, NY: Henry Holt and Company, Inc, 1890, p 416.

25 James underlines the selective nature of perception: "Millions of items of the outward order are present to my senses which never properly enter into my experience. Why? Because they have no *interest* for me. *My experience is what I agree to attend to.* Only those items which I *notice* shape my mind—without selective interest, experience is an utter chaos. Interest alone gives accent and emphasis, light and shade, background and foreground—intelligible perspective, in a word." Ibid, p 402.

26 Another way to put this is to say that beings are 'touched'. American philosopher Judith Butler equates the affective encounter with tactility, and like Merleau-Ponty argues that intelligibility is ultimately disclosed through sentient experience. See Nigel Thrift, "Understanding the Material Practices of Glamour", *The Affect Theory Reader*, Melissa Gregg and Gregory Seigworth, eds, Durham, NC, and London, UK: Duke University Press, 2010, p 303.

However, there is a further dimension to the generation of affect, which relates to one of the word's main derivatives: affection. Solar designs that aim to be affective and relate to the body should also be worthy of affection. There are reasons why we surround ourselves with some things and stay away from others. German philosopher Edmund Husserl refers to such desire for proximity as a "tending-toward".[21] As British-Australian cultural theorist Sara Ahmed explains, "To be affected by something is to evaluate that thing. Evaluations are expressed in how bodies turn toward things. To give value to things is to shape what is near us."[22] Moreover, chosen things that are near fall within a sphere of practical action, "which I can experience in an optimal form through seeing, touching, etc.".[23] In other words, certain artefacts are magnetic because they generate affective interest.[24] Human perception is therefore an active process that involves many mechanisms, some unconscious, some conscious.[25]

Most people experience something as affective when they are attracted to both *it* and *what surrounds it*, which includes the timing of its appearance, location, backdrop and the conditions of its arrival. For example, a person may wish to keep a certain object within reach because somebody they love has given it to them, or because it appeals to their senses. Designers can therefore coax peoples' tendency to assimilate things into their immediate sphere by creating conditions for affective encounters. In the same way, solar designs can create affective connections between sunlight, people and things.[26]

The intelligibility gained from the sensing self is limited, however, since human experience of the world is primarily subjective. As Alice Rawsthorn remarks, "each of us will interpret the affects of the Thonet Chair slightly differently". What matters, then, are the constant, unchanging traits of the thing itself since it is these that allow the Thonet chair to make a powerful impression. Indeed, the design has become an established classic due to its appeal to certain commonalities of human perception, referred to earlier as "parameters"—our awareness of time, temperature, scale and material. For those with knowledge of the history of industrial design, the chair awakens our sense of time; it stimulates the sense of temperature through the "emotional warmth of [its] wood", to use Rawsthorn's words; sense of scale is addressed by the way it fits to the human body, as well as in its scale of production; and the chair's material contributes to its character of novelty as the wood is manipulated in an innovative manner by technology. Hence, established design criteria, as encompassed in the Thonet chair, address many of the fundamental basics of human perception, while also acknowledging aspects of individual history and circumstance.

However, the appeal of the Thonet chair also goes beyond our four principal parameters of perception to address additional associated ones, such as the feeling of reassurance or security that arises from the reliability of the technique used in the chair's manufacture. Although security is not one of the key criteria applied here, it can be linked to the sense of scale (which *is* a key criterion),

"There is a further dimension to the
generation of affect, which relates to one
of the word's main derivatives: affection."

when, for example, it relates to the function of sheltering. A tight, warm and
constricted space may promote a sense of security, especially if placed inside an
open, cold space. Our needs for security and shelter have been linked to
perception of scale ever since human beings resided in small enclosed caves.

Thus, our four principal sensory parameters branch out to intermingle with
and feed off others associated with them. In the case of solar design, the stimuli
that provoke our awareness of time, temperature, scale and material are extracted
in the designs that follow in order to gain a deeper understanding of how sensory
experience may relate to concepts during the process of perception, and how this
can help capture people's affections. While modulating between the natural
and the human environments, these criteria also mark their presence as cultural
constructs by evoking multiple levels of reference, including social relevance and
cultural memory.

The take on affect proposed here also builds on Maurice Merleau-Ponty's
philosophy of embodiment in its focus on three themes: the scientific, the
synaesthetic and the situational. It is the designer's job to foreground these three
themes through the tools at their disposal and the way in which they operate.

The Scientific

In *Structure of Behavior* (1942), Merleau-Ponty discusses how scientific reasoning
in biology and physics connects to sensual perception. Although he does not
deal with the problem directly, he does bring up the relationship between what
can be logically explained and what is physically and psychologically felt. His
discussion of the subject can thus serve as a basis for examining the connections
between physical laws and qualitative design, or, more precisely, the perception
of designs that contain environmentally friendly technologies.

For Merleau-Ponty, the laws of physical systems add a level of precision to lived
experience of the intersubjective world. Thus, a mechanical engineer, for example,
may calculate the thickness of a wall's insulation to determine the efficiency of
the material used and the adequacy of the R-value (the measure of thermal
resistance used in the building industry). Non-engineers may derive satisfaction
from understanding that the dimensions of a wall are not random, but are
instead chosen to keep inhabitants warm without wasting space and material.

According to Merleau-Ponty, then, scientific laws can help conceptualise or
make our understanding of perception more precise. Hence technological
materials such as solar panels, which visibly incorporate the laws of physical
systems, can enable us to better comprehend—after encountering them—the

"Designers can therefore coax peoples'
tendency to assimilate things into their
immediate sphere by creating conditions
for affective encounters."

way in which ideas subsist in matter. Any distinction between the lived and the known is therefore artificial: humans are neither brutes nor analytical systems, and architecture and design can trigger feelings and sensual stimuli in individuals, which in turn generate rational understanding. However, Merleau-Ponty also recognised that biological or physical laws are not what motivate human beings, but, rather, are disembodied afterthoughts. If the technological aspects of the design dominate our view, as they often do in sustainable architecture, they will appear as self-enclosed systems unrelated to context and will disrupt our sensual lived experience.

In *On Span and Space*, Sandaker provides examples of how the structural components of a building can lead to the qualitative enjoyment of architectural space. Referring to the ferro-cement wave forms suspended from the ceiling of Renzo Piano's De Menil Collection in Houston, Texas, he describes them as looking like "white linen hung out to dry; a steady breeze gently pushes the textiles to one side and so admits the soft reflections of the sunlight."[27] In their resemblance to textiles that appear to serve no structural purpose, these elements stimulate the imagination of visitors while modulating light conditions in the museum, and thus perform several design functions simultaneously.

The goal is therefore to ensure that the lived aspects of the design come to the forefront, while the physical laws remain in the background. Hence, while using technology to measure light and temperature, the solar projects presented here aim to use scientific concepts in a way that enables qualitative perception. In doing so, the scientific action of the photovoltaic material takes on emergent qualities connected to either subjective viewpoints or design intents (such as the choice of colour of a specific PV panel according to its context) that do not obey the laws of causality. Ultimately, however, the aim of solar and sustainable design is to arouse human interest on as wide a scale as possible, beyond either sensory pleasure or scientific understanding. In the late 1960s, American architect Richard Neutra explained how amplifying lived sensual experience with technology and scientific analysis could also lead towards heightened environmental awareness:[28] "Our manifold sensory capacities, amplified by our technological instrumentation and sharp scientific analysis, can anticipate and avert the many micro facts of environmental damage."[29] In other words, through offering sensory interaction with the local and wider surroundings, affective, sustainable design might redress society's disregard for the environment to prevent further damage, and push people towards environmental and social responsibility.

27 Sandaker, *On Span and Space*, p 149.

28 "While Neutra is tied with the phenomenological tradition in his fascination with the role played by the human senses in understanding the world, his ideas privilege a more scientific or clinical foundation than the architectural phenomenologists." Michael J Ostwald and Raeana Henderson, "The Modern Interior and the Excitation Response: Richard Neutra's Ocular-centric Phenomenology', *Architecture Research*, 2(3), 2012, pp 27–35.

29 Neutra, Richard, *Nature Near: Late Essays of Richard Neutra*, William Marlin, ed, Santa Barbara, CA: Capra Press, 1989, p 15.

30 "Each sense is a total part freeing a universe that is complete in itself and yet open onto that of the other senses: Each 'sense' is a 'world,' i.e. absolutely incommunicable for the other senses, and yet constructing a *something* which, through its structure, is from the first *open* upon the world of the other senses, and with them forms one sole Being (VI 271/217)." Renaud Barbaras, *The Being of the Phenomenon—Merleau-Ponty's Ontology*, Ted Toadvine and Leonard Lawler, trans, Bloomington and Indianapolis, IN: Indiana University Press, 2004, p 200.

31 Heschong, Lisa, *Thermal Delight in Architecture*, Cambridge, MA: MIT Press, 1979, p 24.

32 Bernard Berenson discusses this phenomenon, as referenced in Juhani Pallasmaa, *The Eyes of the Skin*, London, UK: Academy Editions, 1996, p 44.

33 "The field of inter-involvement ... flows into that between color and sound, in which specific types of sound infect the experience of color, intensifying or dampening it. Words participate in this process, too, as when the word 'hard' produces a stiffening of the back or neck." William E. Connolly, "Materialities of Experience", Melissa Gregg and Gregory Seigworth, eds, *The Affect Theory Reader*, Durham, NC, and London, UK: Duke University Press, 2010, p 182.

34 Neutra, *Nature Near*, p 17.

The Synaesthetic

To understand how to appeal to both the mind and the senses, we can argue that affect is synaesthetic. Synaesthesia is a neurological phenomenon in which the stimulation of one particular sensory or cognitive pathway leads to automatic, involuntary experiences in another.[30] The human body contains millions of sensory receptors that respond to external stimuli and that enable us to see, hear, smell, feel and taste. Although we are conscious that these senses work separately, we are often unaware that they also work together simultaneously—that is, synaesthetically. As American architect and writer Lisa Heschong explains in her critique of ocular centrism:

> One of the magical things about our senses is that they do not function in isolation. Each sense contributes to the fuller comprehension of other sensory information. Indeed, one may not even be able to understand the information from one sense properly until it can be related to information from other senses.[31]

The degree of synaesthesia relates to the generation of affect because the latter requires the senses to participate with each other. By way of example, hanging a photo of a waterfall or similar nature scene in a hot and humid room can help relieve the heat.[32] Similarly, the thermal and visual sensations caused by the cool dark shadow of a solar panel on a glass façade can be reinforced by the sound of wind blowing through a nearby tree. Colour, too, can trigger an affective charge.[33] Interaction between the sensory and cognitive channels can therefore intensify and enrich the perceptual process. Accordingly, the architecture and design discussed in the following chapters rely on tactics that nurture and encode the flow of some intersensory interactions over others. If these flows or 'circuits' are eliminated, then the perceptual experience will likewise diminish. Thus an artificial plant may disappoint because the visual sense is not reinforced by the olfactory and tactile ones; simply put, smell and touch are not encoded into the experience.

Neutra proposes that the ability to perceive or recognise form beyond merely visual or auditory information should be more central to the architect's calling:

> This more implicit and inclusive fusion of sensory experience and response is known as stereognosis [...]. Least of all can architects afford to ignore this stereognostic reality, in which our sensory and spiritual nature is coalesced. A vitality-enhancing environment, providing a regenerative equilibrium between our surroundings and inner life, must be their fundamental objective.[34]

Like synaesthesia, stereognosis, which foregrounds the sense of touch, is mediated by the central nervous system, and is therefore a more complex associative function (people suffering from Alzheimer's, for example, show

35 Huff, FJ, JT Becker, SH Belle, RD Nebes, AL
Holland and F Boller, "Cognitive Deficits and
Clinical Diagnosis of Alzheimer's Disease",
Neurology 37, 1987, pp 1119–1124.

36 Baudelaire, Charles, "Correspondances", *Les Fleurs
du Mal*, Paris: Le Livre de Poche, 1857.

37 Gendlin asks the same question in relation to his
practice in psychotherapy. See Eugene T Gendlin,
review of Maurice Merleau-Ponty's *The Structure
of Behavior*, Alden L Fisher, trans, *The Modern
Schoolman*, 42, 1964, pp 87–96, focusing.org/
gendlin/docs/gol_2091.html, 89, accessed 2
November 2014.

reduced stereognosis).[35] Synaesthesia relates to stereognosis in that it entails the fusion of sensory experience, in which cerebral and bodily pathways reinforce one another. In Neutra's view, architecture that induces stereognostic or haptic perception is therefore more enlivening because it activates multiple senses.

For example, certain design strategies emphasise different environments by enabling viewers or inhabitants to experience those beyond the physical confines of the structures they inhabit. This might include a garden outside a house, where the sound of the wind may coincide with outdoor lights growing brighter. Another way to connect the body to the environment could be by installing an outdoor shower in a sunny spot, thereby providing indoor/outdoor thermal pleasure. Such measures require forethought on the part of the designer, but are neither technically challenging, nor expensive. Through them, the body can immerse itself in forces—local plants, smells and climatic conditions—beyond its immediate environs through synaesthesia. In this way, the body becomes tied to local circumstances and place.

In "Correspondances", the French nineteenth-century poet Charles Baudelaire describes synaesthetic experience as the "ecstasies of mind and senses", induced by a mix of perfumes, colours and sounds in the "temple" of nature.[36] Just as nature evokes sensual correspondences in his poem, so, too, architects and designers can select corresponding perceptions and sensations (perfumes, colours, sounds) and incorporate them into their designs. The sensual stimuli that architects choose to incorporate, however, should be determined by the local environment and appropriate to the task at hand. In the case of solar design, stimuli involving our senses of time, temperature, scale and material are particularly relevant to lived experience and can be manipulated by the designer, through devices such as windows or screens, to shape the manner in which designs are experienced.

However, although the designer may emphasise an individual sense in a given design, it is the degree to which the sensual experiences interrelate that is key to the creation of affect. Rather than distinguishing between object and subject, the aim here is to examine the modes of continuity that exist in given situations and integrate these into the design process. The goal of these interventions is to engage all the senses in holistic experiences that revolve around sunlight. Drawing on Merleau-Ponty, and giving primacy to the lived over the conceptual, this study emphasises the concrete, the felt and the lived synaesthetic experience of the here-and-now. Yet it also asks how concepts can be made to relate to lived experiences without replacing them. In other words, how can one stay true to the lived and yet have concepts?[37]

Let us begin by looking at what Lisa Heschong calls "associated modes of perception". Like the French philosopher Gaston Bachelard, Heschong claims that the most vivid, powerful experiences are those that involve all the senses at once. To illustrate her point, she uses Bachelard's description of watching a fire, whose

"The sensual stimuli that architects choose to incorporate, however, should be determined by the local environment and appropriate to the task at hand."

warmth, smell, sound and flickering light offer multisensory stimulation. Yet fire also brings into play associated modes of perception (smell, for example, is linked to memory) and thus kindles the imagination. As Bachelard notes, "reverie before a burning fire is [...] the first and most truly human use of fire".[38]

In their study, *Body, Memory and Architecture*, Kent Bloomer and Charles Moore point to the absence of the senses and their associated modes of perception in architecture as an ongoing problem:[39]

> What is missing in our dwellings today are the potential transactions between body, imagination and environment [...] to at least some extent every place can be remembered, partly because it is unique, but partly because it has affected our bodies and generated enough associations to hold it in our personal worlds.[40]

Bloomer and Moore were among the first to discuss the ways in which mind-body connections are reinforced by multisensory experiences in architecture. Merleau-Ponty describes perception in a similar manner, pointing out that it entails an intermingling of things, eyes, hands and mind in which vision is a thought that decodes bodily signals: "Vision is not the metamorphosis of the things themselves in their vision [...] It's a thought that deciphers strictly the signs given in the body."[41]

Merleau-Ponty also describes the way in which directly felt experience interacts with concepts such as ethical responsibility, a view influenced by the ideas of the French Cartesian philosopher Nicolas Malebranche, who illustrated that intelligibility merged with lived experience and the senses, and that this in turn could lead to an ethical response.[42] Similarly, certain psychotherapists try to enable their patients to respond more appropriately and ethically to their own circumstances by creating better understanding of mind/body connections. For example, in collaboration with psychologist Carl Rogers, and inspired by Merleau-Ponty's philosophy, American philosopher and psychologist Eugene T Gendlin conducted a series of studies where he and Rogers taught patients how to refer to their felt senses and then measured the extent to which they did so.[43] In this sense, their objective was similar to that of the architect/designer who helps clients connect the lived with the conceptual realm.

As used here, the term 'affect' builds on Gendlin's understanding of Merleau-Ponty, in seeing senses as functioning in relation to concepts so they can mutually reinforce one another. Hence designers can use tactics to encourage people to both feel and understand architectural spaces. By integrating sunlight into the

38 Heschong, *Thermal Delight*, p 29.

39 Bloomer, Kent C, and Charles Moore, *Body, Memory, and Architecture*, New Haven, CT: Yale University Press, 1977.

40 As referenced in Pallasmaa, *The Eyes of the Skin*, p 41.

41 Merleau-Ponty, Maurice, *L'Œil et l'Esprit*, Paris: Éditions Gallimard, 1964, p 41: "Des choses aux yeux et des yeux à la vision il ne se passe rien de plus que des choses aux mains de l'aveugle et de ses mains à sa pensée. La vision n'est pas la métamorphose des choses mêmes en leur vision, la double appartenance des choses au grand monde et à un petit monde privé. C'est une pensée qui déchiffre strictement les signes donnés dans le corps."

42 See American philosopher Judith Butler for further elaboration of Merleau-Ponty's ideas and the role of Malebranche: "The ethical does not primarily describe conduct or disposition, but characterizes a way of understanding the relational framework within which sense, action and speech become possible. The ethical describes a structure of address in which we are called upon to act or to respond in a specific way." Judith Butler, *Senses of the Subject*, New York, NY: Fordham University Press, 2015, p 41.

43 Gendlin, Eugene T, *Focusing*, New York, NY: Bantam Books, 2007, p X, focusing.org, accessed 4 November 2014.

"The designer'
and provoke relati
and situations
centred in the b
are born from sen
reflect individua
the givens

ask is to select

s between people

Because they are

y, these relations

al perceptions that

bodily mood and

f the milieu."

"By integrating sunlight into the
solar designs, both the sensual
and affective aspects of this light,
together with awareness of its
abstract laws and eco-ethical
implications, can be underscored."

solar designs, both the sensual and affective aspects of this light, together with awareness of its abstract laws and eco-ethical implications, can be underscored. To illustrate this (as will be discussed in Chapter 3), the thermal experience of walking down a corridor in Cocoon House is enhanced by colours, each of which adds meaning to the experience. As sunlight pours in through translucent coloured panels above,[44] the feeling of warmth on the skin gives rise to thermal pleasure, which is reinforced by colour, which in turn is reinforced by that colour's symbolic connotations. The coloured skylights that surmount the corridor derive their meaning from the paintings of the British Romantic landscape painter William Turner, which are based on German writer Johann Wolfgang von Goethe's colour theory. Crimson, for example, alludes to evening and rest, while yellow signals the sun at its zenith or midday activity. Any encounter with these skylights will therefore be more affective because the senses of temperature, colour, scale and time, as well as the cerebral structures associated with their colour symbolism and how it relates to the home's circulation pattern, are all activated and engaged. At the same time, the enjoyment of warmth and other sensory experience derived from the skylights translates into an emotional experience of wellbeing. The red light passing through the red skylight, for instance, signals and recalls sunset in one's mind, which triggers a restful mind/body response. Thus when light is filtered through apertures designed to amplify its sensual and cognitive appeal, a strong synaesthetic and affective reaction will be engendered, and the energy and eco-ethical implications of the sun will be felt that much more keenly.

Photovoltaic panels can, then, be integrated into architecture and design so that they respond to ecological forces and the environment as it relates to the body, its senses, and cognition, including collective conscience. The fact that visitors can perceive and feel these panels transforming the sun's energy into power, thereby reducing the cosmic scale to the human, adds another affective layer to the perceptive process. In its experience of sunlight at different latitudes and times of day, the human body thus takes centre stage, just as it does in Merleau-Ponty's philosophy of embodiment. If, on the other hand, photovoltaic panels are tacked onto a design as an afterthought, as often happens, they will most likely lack sensual appeal and be perceived as inert, self-enclosed systems 'from without', rather than lively connective materials 'from within'.

44 These coloured skylights will ultimately be photovoltaic and therefore produce energy, but the company contracted to supply them, Onyx from Spain, pulled out at the last minute due to the difficulty of getting UL (Underwriters Laboratories) rating in the US. The discussion of such panels throughout this book is therefore based on their potential, rather than actual, effect when installed in the house.

45 Connolly, "Materialities of Experience", p 182.

46 "A felt sense is the many-stranded fabric of bodily awareness that (for example) guides golfers as they tee off. It would be impossible for them to *think* all the details of location, surrounding environment, and body movement that are woven into aiming." Gendlin, *Focusing*, p 96.

47 Merleau-Ponty quoted by Eugene T Gendlin, review of Maurice Merleau-Ponty's *The Structure of Behavior*, in *The Modern Schoolman*, pp 87–96, focusing.org/gendlin/docs/gol_2091.html, accessed 5 November 2014.

48 Leatherbarrow, David, *Uncommon Ground— Architecture, Technology and Topography*, Cambridge, MA, and London, UK: MIT Press, 2000, p 66.

The Situational

The designer's task is to select and provoke relations between people and situations. Because they are centred in the body, these relations are born from sensual perceptions that reflect individual bodily mood and the givens of the milieu. In a two-way transaction between milieu and body, the body assumes a "spatiality of situation", as Merleau-Ponty writes, quoted here by Connolly:

> Most importantly, the act of perception is permeated by implicit reference to the position and mood of one's own body in relation to the phenomenal field [...] indeed [the body's] spatiality is not [...] a *spatiality of position* but a *spatiality of situation*.[45]

Felt behaviour is always 'in the world',[46] and the designer can influence the impact of different milieus by shaping how they relate to people. For example, each time the photovoltaic material is applied to a new design, it takes on a new role in the overall composition. The challenge of the design process is therefore to find a material language that is fitting to each new design and situation.

However, the relationship between body and surroundings is also symbiotic, which by definition entails mutual advantageousness. The designer orchestrates the manner in which the environment relates to the human body, and, in turn, humans reorganise the environment that surrounds them according to embedded patterns in their natures: "[T]he animal organism constructs a stable milieu for itself corresponding to the [...] embedded patterns of need and instinct [...]. Behavior [...] is related to [...] the environment proper to each species and to each individual."[47] The "environment proper" to humans is thus a function of how they reorganise it, which engenders a "spatiality of situation", in a two-way transaction between milieu and body. David Leatherbarrow describes this phenomenon with reference to Neutra: "One's body has in its interior darkness not only abilities but also inclinations or predispositions of posture, which Neutra called kinesthetic patterns. These reciprocate what is saturated in the fittings, materials, and dimensions of a setting."[48]

Designers can lay the ground for relationships between human beings and their environments, but, above all, the world in which the body is immersed can be designed for the senses to help trigger affective encounters (for example, sitting habitually in the same chair because it receives evening sun). These encounters can be contained, whittled, or channelled, as well as modulated by the uniqueness of the context and the people who inhabit it. For instance, in the example used in the previous section (also discussed in Chapter Three), a bedroom corridor is surmounted by translucent coloured skylights, which can be enhanced by contained affects. The yellow skylight, signalling the zenith of the sun, or midday, is placed closest to the living area, the most active space of the house. The affect of this yellow colour comprises three elements—brightness, saturation and hue—though these may vary

"The scientific, synaesthetic and situational aspects of solar design can all be employed in the generation of affect."

depending on the light quality of the day (becoming more intense on a sunny day when the sunlight hits the yellow panel directly), and the inhabitant's mood and personal history. In this particular case, the inhabitant's familiarity with the paintings of Turner, upon which the colour scheme is based, is also particularly relevant.

Time, Temperature, Scale and Material

The scientific, synaesthetic and situational aspects of solar design can all be employed in the generation of affect. Each of the criteria discussed in the previous chapter—time, temperature, scale and material—gravitates towards one of these concepts. For example, the photovoltaic material relates to the scientific, sense of temperature to the synaesthetic, and sense of scale to the situational, all of which are interrelated. The sense of time, which relates to the solar clock, embraces all three concepts because the body senses time in time, *as time*.

Time

Of the four criteria, the sense of time is most deeply connected to affect, as affect can only be experienced in time. In other words, affect, which necessarily involves a person's attraction towards an object, can be defined as a form of continuity, a constant motion. In her essay "The Affective Turn", Patricia Clough notes that the passage of time is registered neurophysiologically, a fraction of a second at a time. However, design can expand our consciousness of time, by creating affective encounters that take place over different and repeated timescales. Firstly, solar designs can stimulate affective synaesthetic experiences in *present* time by awakening multiple senses and generating associations between them. Secondly, designers can draw attention to *cyclical* time by referring to and accentuating light play. And thirdly, by contrasting new and weathered materials, designers can heighten people's awareness of the passage of *linear* time.

The intention of the designs presented in the following chapters is to use technologies that respond to the sun's movement and energy. For example, the movement and intensity of the sun, and its diurnal and seasonal cycles, are experienced through devices that create animated patterns during the daytime, and illumination at dusk. Their solar modules, which are programmed to automatically turn on at dusk, are visibly exposed in order to reveal the electrical engineering of the LEDs and remind the viewer of the rhythmical flow of solar energy. By such means, solar design can counteract the "indefinite intensification" of the digital age,[49] as well as contemporary society's loss of connection to planetary movements. As artist James Turrell writes:

49 Picon, Antoine, *Digital Culture in Architecture, an Introduction for the Design Professions*, Basel, Switzerland: Birkhauser, 2010, p 202.

50 *James Turrell*, Fundacion NMAC, Milan, Italy: Edizioni Charta, 2009, p 35.

51 Picon, *Digital Culture in Architecture*, p 202.

52 Laurent Beaudouin, quoted in *Sensing Spaces— Architecture Reimagined*, London, UK: Royal Academy Publications, 2014, p 83.

53 Mostafavi, Mohsen and David Leatherbarrow, *On Weathering—The Life of Buildings in Time*, London, UK, and Cambridge, MA: The MIT Press, 1993, p 84.

There was a time when men were very much aware of the solar movement, the stars, the sun [...] the calendars of different civilizations such as the Mayans, the Egyptians and even the Christians were related to the positions and movements of the planets. We live in a time where we have lost this connection with the earth and the sky.[50]

Of course, today's awareness of planetary movements will never match that of ancient civilisations. But arguably, society is even losing its connection to the senses, including its sense of the passage of time. Ever-increasing digital screen-time spent in a fast-paced, reactive mode distracts people from reflecting on past and future. Historian of architecture and technology Antoine Picon and others have criticised the architecture of the age of the internet for its immersion in a "seeming never-ending present" and for its lack of memory.[51]

The French architect Laurent Beaudouin also writes about the differences of time experienced in the human, natural and architecture worlds, suggesting these can be reconciled through design: "Human time moves quickly, and architecture can be a means of slowing time down, allowing the human to become more in tune with the natural."[52] Incorporating the felt presence of the sun into a building, for example, could slow down time through inducing reflection and observation— the sun as read by both body and mind.

A designer's ability to promote a sense of continuity from past to future could therefore offer audiences a richer perspective. One way that designs could reference the past is by incorporating weathered materials and traditional technologies that evolved from local conditions and cultures, while addressing the future by promoting sustainability. For example, when combined with traditional local materials such as cedar shingles, photovoltaic panels might provide a valuable contrast between different technologies, and heighten awareness of links between past and future. David Leatherbarrow and Iranian-American architect and educator Mohsen Mostafavi have written about the value of ageing surfaces: "[D]iscussion of 'age value' can be identified with [...] the idea that the various markings and layers of a surface record [...] earlier stages in the history of a building (or design) and the human life associated with it."[53]

The use of ageing materials to represent the history of humanity and its interaction with the environment is also exemplified in the work of Spanish architect and artist Jorge Otero-Pailos. In his installation of 2016, *Ethics of Dust*, he wrapped latex over the stones of the eastern internal wall of Westminster Hall in the Houses of Parliament, in London. The latex created a translucent skin (50m long x 6m high) that absorbed dust over three days to form what the artist called a "skin of history", drawing attention to the microscopic layers of sediment that had settled on the wall for almost two centuries, and prompting people to think about the stories and histories embodied in them. Otero-Pailos claims that, in addition to serving as a record of the world, this work can help us look to the future:

54 Abrams, Amah-Rose, "Artangel and Jorge Otero-Pailos Will Cast the Houses of Parliament in Latex", artnet.com, accessed 23 May 2016.

55 Harries, "What Need is There for Environmental Aesthetics?" p 16.

56 Connolly, "Materialities of Experience", p 184.

57 Heschong, *Thermal Delight*, p 38.

58 Ahmed, Sara, *Queer Phenomenology—Orientations, Objects, Others*, Durham, NC: Duke University Press, 2006, p 9.

The rocks that are being formed today are different to those that were formed one thousand years ago when Westminster Hall was built [...]. For me it is really important that we think about time in a more expanded way [...] to think what we want to share across generations. It's important that we have that conversation.[54]

In a similar way, perceptive encounters with environmental technologies such as photovoltaic panels may help us understand our place in time, including our future, as well as man's relationship with nature. By enhancing transitory bodily perceptions of sunlight, and heightening awareness of the generation of electric power, these panels may also play a role in mitigating global warming. As Karsten Harries writes:

[T]he meaning of our individual death-bound lives depends crucially on our ability to place ourselves in an ongoing community. And if so, would we not want, or rather, feel a duty towards making sure that the environment will continue to speak to us of such a faith in the future?[55]

By paying respect to cultural memory, architecture and design therefore have the potential to articulate past, present and future of an ongoing community. As William Connolly notes in reference to Merleau-Ponty: "Perception not only has multiple layers of intersensory *memory* folded into it, it is suffused with *anticipation*."[56] The artefacts presented in this book attempt to concretise these aspects of time while using material and light as measures.

Temperature

Solar designs can embody different temperatures as well as temporalities. When people are asked to name a heating or cooling object, the first thing that usually comes to mind is a radiator or fan. The designs here attempt to build on the simple thermal function of such objects, by stimulating the thermal, tactile and visual senses all at once—synaesthaetically.

Solar architecture and design enhance the sun's warmth by connecting the senses of temperature, colour and touch. The designs' tactile surfaces, whether made of rusted steel, textile or wood, are textured and thus reinforce their users' sense of temperature. Whenever we touch something, we immediately register information about its temperature, regardless of whether we are aware of it.[57] An affection for objects may therefore derive partly from this enjoyment of their warmth, or coolness, to the touch. As Sara Ahmed explains:

As it is affected and shaped by its surroundings, the skin [...] is also where the atmosphere creates an impression; just think of goose bumps, textures on the skin surface, as body traces of the coldness of the air. Bodies may become orientated in this responsiveness to the world around them, given this capacity to be affected.[58]

59 The closed stove is the result of a gradual changeover from radiant to convective heating systems. As we start to understand the building as an airtight enclosure for warm air, we gradually replace the fireplace with the closed stove and the solar heating functions of the building. Heschong, *Thermal Delight*, p 14.

60 Ibid, p viii.

61 Bachelard, Gaston, *La Poétique de l'Espace (The Poetics of Space)—The Classic Look at How We Experience Intimate Places*, Paris: Presses Universitaires de France, 1958, p 41.

Moreover, warmth to the touch often reinforces warmth of colour because temperature relates to colour. Hot items radiate light, like the filament of an incandescent bulb, for example, and its temperature affects the colour of this light. As colour perception is linked to temperature perception, the sight of warm colour tones such as red can give rise to pleasurable feelings of warmth. Even with 'cool' lights like LEDs, temperature can be sensed indirectly through their colour, as such lights emit a warm tone that reminds viewers of the heated energy of the sun that powers them.

Some of the solar works designed for cold climates generate warmth in both the abstract and physical sense of the word, through conduction, ambient temperature and colour, all of which can induce feelings of welcome and contentment. For example, when comparing a closed stove to an open fireplace in terms of its capacity to convey warmth, a fireplace radiates heat directly, but a closed convection stove directs hot air upwards and circulates it indirectly around the room. Can this reduced amount of heat directed at the body lead to a weaker experience of warmth? Although the closed stove is more energy efficient than the fireplace,[59] does it improve on the amount of heat generated by the open fireplace in ways that are not merely quantitative? As Lisa Heschong writes, "With its circle of warmth, the fireplace had once been the center of family life. Its dancing light, smoky smells and warm crackling created an ambience that made a house more a home."[60] The warmth emitted by the traditional fireplace therefore induces sensual and cognitive wellbeing on many levels. By contrast, the sensual pleasure offered by the closed stove is compromised by the absence of sounds, smells and immediate radiation to the body. Does this reduced sensual stimulation also result in fewer feelings of wellbeing associated with the conventional fireplace, including the power to evoke memories? In French author Henri Bachelin's description of the winters he spent in his father's house, he noted that storytelling and remembrance were both heightened by the presence of the fireplace.[61]

The solar designs discussed in the following pages aim to stimulate thermal sensations and provide warmth/refreshment in a synaesthetic and affective manner, much as Bachelin's fireplace does. They may not capture the senses in the same way as a lit fireplace or a forest in flames, but they have the potential to touch the senses and to engage the user both physically and emotionally.

Scale

In addition to offering an enriched sense of time and "thermal delight" (Heschong's term), the solar works discussed here are designed to embody a layered sense of scale, in which the global, the local and the human scales coexist, generated by the body's physical positions and psychological states, and the particularities of the space and context. Thinking along these lines may reshape our usual notions about how we inhabit space. As David Leatherbarrow notes:

"Designers can la
relationships betw
and their environr
the world in which
can be designed fo
trigger affectiv

he ground for
en human beings
nts, but above all,
he body is immersed
the senses to help
encounters."

62 Leatherbarrow, *Uncommon Ground*, p 66.

63 Charles and Ray Eames, "Powers of Ten: A Film Dealing with the Relative Size of Things in the Universe and the Effect of Adding Another Zero", 1977, based on the book *Cosmic View*, 1957, by Dutch educator Kees Boeke.

When we rethink customary notions of space [...] we begin to see that this corporeal schema is enmeshed within an expanding range of distances [...] that includes where I am [...] a middle distance, and an expansion toward the clear blue horizon [...]. Not one of these can be separated from the others, hence the lateral spread of an ensemble that integrates these "rings" into one field, terrain or topography—the dining room, the street, and the town or landscape [...].[62]

Designers can draw attention to these "rings" by relating their materials and geometry to the human, local, global and solar scales all at once. They can address the human scale, the central point of reference, by attempting synaesthesia, by stimulating, to a greater or lesser extent, the senses of temperature, hearing, touch and sight. Many of the artefacts here are made of raw local materials that also underscore the local scale, and light up according to seasonal rhythms during cyclical energy-forming processes. At the same time, some of the photovoltaic panels are mirrored and reflect the clouds and greenery of the surroundings, while also being angled towards the sun's rays for optimal solar collection. Finally, the micro scale of the chemical processes inherent in the material is indicated by metallic stripes, or crystallised patterns, on the photovoltaic panel. This stark contrast between the molecular and cosmic scales apparent in the material surface and the angle of the panel show us how the micro and macro scales can collapse into one another.

The solar works discussed in this volume approach scale much as Charles and Ray Eames do in *Powers of Ten* (1977).[63] This short film depicts the relative scale of the universe according to an order of magnitude based on a factor of ten—zooming out from the Earth to the entire universe, then zooming in to a single atom. In a similar vein, the American land artist Robert Smithson managed to arouse our sense of multiple scales in his famous land work of 1970, *Spiral Jetty*. Constructed out of black basalt rocks and earth from the Great Salt Lake into which the jetty projects, the installation consists, at a micro level, of millions of microscopic salt crystals, whose spiral forms reflect the overall megastructure in miniature.

Above all, as mediators of natural light, solar designs direct attention to the vast nurturing power of the sun, which could potentially inspire a more positive attitude to the relationship between technology and nature. Today we no longer equate the sun with human reason as did the philosophers of the Enlightenment, or view it as an immense natural force that overwhelms us to the point of helplessness, as did the poets of the Romantic era. Instead, we perceive the sun and solar energy in terms of the relations between humans, technology and nature, and see environmental technologies such as solar panels as offering a way to cooperate with powerful natural forces.

Photovoltaic panels, then, engender a sense of connection with the distant solar system at multiple levels—at local environmental and molecular levels

"Today's awareness of planetary
movements will never match that
of ancient civilisations. But arguably,
society is even losing its connection
to the senses, including its sense of
the passage of time."

through their reflective surfaces, and with the sun through their latitudinal tilt (the panels are tilted at a lower angle in southern locations, where the sun is higher in the sky, and at a higher angle in northern locations, where it is lower). The designer can try to increase this legibility of scale by engaging the evolving, interconnected matter of the panels' surroundings through strategies that will be described in greater detail in the following chapters.

Material

Exploration of new types and uses of materials drives the design of the artefacts presented here. For example, photovoltaic glass, one of the most rapidly developing architectural materials today,[64] belongs to the new material culture of sustainable architecture and design. However, the conventional use of this technology needs to be re-evaluated to enhance its affective potential, which is often eclipsed by its power to generate energy.

In his introduction to *Water and Dreams*, Bachelard claims that there are two imagining powers in our minds, which develop around two different axes.[65] Some get their impetus from novelty, while others seek the primitive and eternal, as summarised in the foreword to his *Poetics of Space*: "The formal imagination is fond of novelty, picturesqueness, variety and unexpectedness in events, while the material imagination is attracted to the element of permanency present in things."[66] Ideally, a material assemblage should appeal to both of Bachelard's forms of imagination. Although photovoltaic surfaces are usually regarded as serving a purely technological function, they can also incorporate aspects of novelty and change that grant artefacts an element of surprise and liveliness, while also becoming a seemingly permanent part of their surroundings. But in order for solar projects to relate affectively to both the material and formal imaginations, as per Bachelard's theory, they need to relate to external *geographical*[67] agencies such as culture and climate, as well as to timeless architectural typologies. For instance, a traditional classical assembly of materials could provide a counterpoint to the sensual play with sunlight of the material itself. Moreover, materials often relate to the emotional rootedness of the home, which may be linked to the sense of identity. As ever greater numbers of global technologies, such as solar-powered portable battery chargers, enter domestic space, the effect of these may become increasingly problematic if they fail to incorporate local crafts and traditions from which the sense of rootedness derives.

64 "The team-up of solar and glass specialists builds a link between glass providers and the fastest growth factor in glass applications today—solar technology. Some of the newest key technologies, such s BIPV (Building Integrated Photovoltaics) offer tremendous potential to cut peak loads of energy loads in buildings." Jorma Vitkala, "Know-How Spurs Growth", in Glass Performance Days 2009, Conference Proceedings, Tampere, Finland, p 3.

65 Bachelard, Gaston, *Water and Dreams: An Essay on the Imagination of Matter* (1942), Dallas, TX: The Pegasus Foundation, 1983.

66 Bachelard, Gaston, *The Poetics of Space—The Classic Look at How We Experience Intimate Places*, Boston, MA: Beacon Press, 1994 edition, foreword, p xiii.

67 I use the term 'geographic' in relation to 'modern geography', "an all-encompassing discipline that foremost seeks to understand the Earth and all of its human and natural complexities […] Geography has been called 'the world discipline' and 'the bridge between the human and the physical science'." en.m.wikipedia.org, accessed 2 April 2014.

68 Addington, Michelle and Daniel Schodek, *Smart Materials and Technologies—For the Architecture and Design Professions*, Oxford, UK, and Burlington, MA: Elsevier, 2005, p 64.

69 Beaudouin, Laurent, *Pour une Architecture Lente*, Paris: Quintette Éditions, 2007.

70 *Sensing Spaces—Architecture Reimagined*, p 83.

71 Picon, *Digital Culture in Architecture*, p 12.

Photovoltaic material and its design potential. Solar design and architecture remain inert until the designer finds potential aspects of novelty and permanence that can be expressed by them. Physicists look at the environment as an energy field in which boundaries are transitional states, subject to changes on the microscopic level. Materials can potentially transform energy as well as alter humidity indexes, luminosity levels, scents, temperature gradients, air masses and plant physiology—in other words, they generate constant novelty. For example, in *Smart Materials and New Technologies*, architect Michelle Addington and engineer Daniel Schodeck describe the problem of aerodynamic lift, attributed by physicists to the subtle and often microscopic changes that occur on the surface of the airfoil, which can significantly alter the boundary between the atmosphere and the airplane wing.[68]

Like physicists, designers of solar artefacts see materials as generative and transitional rather than inert, as actively engaging with their situations and with other materials. In addition, the active boundaries of solar artefacts enable them to relate to the situations in which they exist *over time*. The French architect Laurent Beaudouin, author of *Pour une Architecture Lente* (For a Slow Architecture),[69] writes about the differences of time experienced in the human, natural and architecture worlds: "Human time moves quickly, and architecture can be a means of slowing time down, allowing the human to become more in tune with the natural."[70] The felt presence of the sun could, for example, induce a state of reflection and observation, a pleasurable sensation that slows perception of time—the sun as read by both body and mind. Rather than being limited to its inherent properties therefore, connective photovoltaic matter integrated into design acts as an open-ended, continually producing, absorbing, giving and receiving technology.

As we have seen earlier, photovoltaic panels can also be immersed in their surroundings to absorb and reflect light in ways that reinforce synaesthesia, which, in turn, awakens our perception of energy. For example, when we encounter a solar artefact whose panel is obstructed by the shadow of a tree, we respond to both the shadow and the fact that the solar panel is losing the capacity to absorb energy. If it happens to be a hot and bright day, we may find the cool dark shadow refreshing, a respite from the heat and glare, a reaction that may increase our awareness of how sunlight is absorbed into the energy-rich solar glass. This awareness of synaesthetic perception is one of many affects that can result from the designer's skilful conduction of light.

The solar panels discussed in this book are merely one new type of material that has emerged on the market since the dawn of the digital age. As Picon observes, "The development of digital culture is inseparable from a major transformation of our definition of materiality, at the intersection of technological possibilities and sensory evidence."[71] A new material culture of pixelated and animated surfaces, such as reactive bio-metals on façades, may not just stimulate

72 Thrift, "Understanding the Material Practices of Glamour", p 290.

73 Terreform, a non-profit architectural firm located at New Lab in the Brooklyn navy yard, led by Mitchell Joachim, Melanie Fessel and Maria Aialova, designed the prototype for a lounge chair grown from mushrooms. Ecovative, awarded the Buckminster Fuller 2013 design competition, develops the material.

74 Massumi, Brian, *Parables for the Virtual, Movement, Affect, Sensation*, Durham, NC, and London, UK: Duke University Press, 2002, pp 20–21.

75 Savage, Lynne, "Artificial Photosynthesis—Saving Solar Energy for a Rainy Day", *Optics and Photonic News*, February 2013, p 25.

76 Coole, Diana and Samantha Frost, eds, *New Materialisms—Ontology, Agency, and Politics*, Durham, NC, and London, UK: Duke University Press, 2010, p 20.

77 "Agency may either be classified as unconscious, involuntary behavior, or purposeful, goal directed activity (intentional action). An agent typically has some sort of immediate awareness of his physical activity and the goals that the activity is aimed at realizing." wikipedia.org, accessed 1 November 2013.

78 exeter.edu/libraries/553_4376.aspx, accessed 17 December 2013.

our senses, but also capture our imagination, as in Bachelard's concept of formal imagination, through an entirely new set of affective devices—"new kinds of cultural nerves".[72] In addition, a host of 'green' and 'bio' materials[73] are now becoming available that merge technology with matter and that have contributed to debates surrounding a "new materialism".[74] For example, certain synthetic semiconducting polymers derived from phenylene vinylene can be used as light harvesters for solar energy that imitate photosynthesis performed by natural systems.[75] Many of these new materialist ontologies take a posthumanist stance, as defined by Diana Coole and Samantha Frost:

> There is increasing agreement here that all bodies, including those of animals (and perhaps certain machines too), evince certain capacities for agency. As a consequence, the human species, and the qualities of self-reflection, self-awareness, and rationality traditionally used to distinguish it from the rest of nature, may now seem little more than contingent and provisional forms or processes within a broader evolution or cosmic productivity.[76]

If bodies—including materials—endowed with the sort of agency implied above can trigger "self-reflection, self-awareness and rationality", then materials can potentially act in a goal-orientated fashion.[77] For example, if a solar panel had agency, could it aim at maximum performance, such as trying to tilt to the optimum angle? Or would it simply reflect on and accept the angle in which it has been placed? Is the solar panel capable of such intentionality and conscious self-reflection?

Rather than discussing bodies' capacity for agency, as some posthumanist theorists do, this study examines their capacity for *liveliness*, and the ability of designers to organise bodies in a manner to enhance this. The crux of its argument is that solar artefacts become affective only if designers choose and shape their material choices to connect them to people and their surroundings. American architect Louis Kahn used to tell his students that they should ask their materials for advice: "I asked the brick, 'What do you like, brick?' And brick said, 'I like an arch'."[78] Hence the discussion here revolves around the question of how human agency can enable sustained reflective consciousness through design.

A 'live' material illuminates the solar works in question invisibly and silently. The quasi-living photovoltaic surface captures sunlight with its semiconductor properties and turns it into direct electrical current, but some solar pieces light up automatically at dusk without the help of switches or wires, as if living a life of their own. This hidden source of liveliness, merging machine and organism may enhance their affective potential because of the blurring of boundaries between living and nonliving surfaces. British social scientist and geographer Nigel Thrift claims that one reason we are attracted to certain modern consumer goods is our ability to understand their surfaces as neither inert nor active:

"As mediators of natural light, solar designs
direct attention to the vast nurturing power
of the sun, which could potentially inspire
a more positivist attitude to the relationship
between technology and nature."

> [B]ecause of their uncertain status, they [the surfaces of material goods, such as,
> for example, diamond rings] are able to fascinate, that is, to stimulate explorations
> of their nature and character because they are able to arouse repeated interest
> or stimulate curiosity.[79]

If the conditions of matter and human perception have no fixed identities and
are continually evolving, then energy production can be understood in ways
beyond the 'solar panel' signifier that defines how many kilowatts of electricity
per hour it is able to generate.[80] This means that if the photovoltaic panel is
liberated from its fixed definition and turned into a forever altering material, it
may trigger synaesthetic perception. Neutra notes that a new, lively materialism
is on the rise in architecture:

> In recent decades, our understanding of matter, and accordingly of materials, has
> undergone cognitive as well as connotational change. All of the sciences are
> disclosing that matter is dynamically infused with all manner of significance, from
> the sensorial and spiritual, to the psychological and philosophical.[81]

This view of materiality suggests that it can embrace variety, novelty, and
permanence, and therefore falls into line with Bachelard's paradigm, as
discussed above (p 25). If we are to accept Neutra and Bachelard's premise,
designers should therefore be able to view materials as regenerative yet stable,
connected yet distinct. In the case of photovoltaic material, it could be capable
of simultaneously providing electric power, conducting sunlight, generating
thermal sensations and developing patina. In other words, its fluctuating
sensual and cognitive properties could be contrasted with its known and
immutable qualities (such as the amount of electric power a PV material
provides), and, by drawing out these characteristics, the designer could create
the conditions for a more affective experience of design.

The Felt Sense

According to thinkers such as Merleau-Ponty, change takes place when the
sensual and cognitive impact of affective encounters is combined: when the
bodily senses are awakened, the cognitive powers are likewise aroused, and
perception, including the perception of energy processes, becomes more

79 Thrift, "Understanding the Material Practices of
Glamour", p 296.

80 Hélène Frichot writes about this conceptual shift:
"The claim this essay forwards is that humans and
non-humans alike, inclusive of their architectural
environments, are composed amidst vibrant
material ecologies. This argument takes its cue
from such thinkers as Jane Bennett, Bruno Latour,
Nigel Thrift, Gilles Deleuze, and Felix Guattari,
amongst others, and enlists concepts all of
which share qualities of emergence, including
becoming, assemblage, relationality, and
(importantly for the purposes of this essay), a
politics of affect." Hélène Frichot, "The Stockholm
Bubble—Material Assemblages and Ecologies of
Affect", *Nordic Journal of Architecture*, vol 2, no 3,
winter 2012, p 40.

81 Neutra, *Nature Near*, p 63.

82 As Gendlin describes Merleau-Ponty's views on the relations between abstract laws and lived experience: "Lived perception […] is prior to number, measure, space and causality […] Yet it is through lived perception that we grasp "the intersubjective world, the determinations of which science is gradually making precise". "Science makes precise that which is not given precisely. Therefore no causal power can be attributed to laws. They are retrospective thoughts, afterthoughts." Gendlin, review of Merleau-Ponty's *The Structure of Behavior,* in *The Modern Schoolman,* pp 87–96, 219, focusing.org/gendlin/docs/gol_2091.html, accessed 7 November 2014.

83 Gendlin, *Focusing,* p 191.

84 Harries, "What Need Is There for Environmental Aesthetics?", pp 20, 801.

powerful and precise.[82] Gendlin describes this heightened sensory awareness as a "felt sense", which functions as an extension of the body and leads to analysis and logic.[83] In the case of solar design, this sense arises from the photovoltaic material's relation to a unique situation.

Walter Benjamin believed that if technology became too powerful it risked "reduc[ing] human beings to human material".[84] For Merleau-Ponty, however, when ideas interact with directly felt experience, they become grounded and comprehensible to the human mind rather than abstract. For example, although climate change is still understood mainly through data charts, its effects are increasingly experienced in real physical terms, thanks to erratic temperature levels and natural catastrophes such as Hurricane Sandy, the largest Atlantic hurricane on record. Just a decade ago global warming seemed too abstract a concept to upset most people; today this is much less of a problem.

A "felt sense", then, understood here as the experience of an affective encounter, occurs when a design spurs a visceral connection, when it arouses the senses, meaning and ideas simultaneously, and when it makes the senses of time, temperature, scale and material depend on each other, and thus generate affect. A design fails to be affective when one of these senses is absent or has been compromised. The text that follows focuses on solar designs in which reflective and energy-rich surfaces instigate a relationship between nature, technology and perception. Through these we will investigate the chief characteristics of the perception of sunlight and its consequences in architecture and design.

Chapter Two
THINGS

Thingness

1 Ingold, Tim, "Bringing Things to Life: Creative Entanglements in a World of Materials", Working Paper 15, Scotland, UK: Department of Anthropology, University of Aberdeen, 2010, p 6.

2 Such as those referred to in the Introduction and set out in Coole and Frost, *New Materialisms*.

3 Ingold, "Bringing Things to Life", p 12.

In this chapter, I will distinguish between solar *objects* and solar *things*. Whereas the former are self-contained, the latter are connective and inspire affection; 'thingness' is therefore prioritised over 'objectness'. My four criteria for affective thingness—the appeal to the senses of time, temperature, scale and material—must all be present in the works under discussion to varying degrees. An example of such a thing would be a tree, which changes with the seasons, grows, filters light and shadow, bends and rustles with the wind, thrives in particular locations, performs photosynthesis and drinks water. By interacting with the environment on many levels simultaneously, a tree stimulates the senses of time, temperature, scale and material. The things identified here also aim to become objects of affection, as well as sites of action in a manner similar to a tree, while collecting energy from the sun. And although things that incorporate solar cells are not living like a tree, they are *lively*, in that, unlike inanimate and passive objects, they connect with human perception and presence. Like trees, they negotiate with human beings by involving multiple overlapping fields and happenings simultaneously, as described by social anthropologist Tim Ingold:

> The tree is not an object at all, but a certain gathering together of the threads of life. That is what I mean by a thing [...] The object stands before us as a *fait accompli*, presenting its congealed, outer surfaces to our inspection [...] The thing, by contrast, is a 'going on', or better, a place where several goings on become entwined.[1]

I believe that new theories on the agency of materials[2] partly stem from awareness of the plethora of self-contained, dead objects that characterise contemporary Western surroundings, and the lack of those that embody life processes:

> I suggest that the problem of agency is born of the attempt to re-animate a world of things already deadened or rendered inert by arresting the flows of substance that give them life. In the EWO (Earth Without Objects), things move and grow because they are alive, not because they have agency. And they are alive precisely because they have not been reduced to the status of objects.[3]

4 Merleau-Ponty, Maurice, *The Primacy of Perception*, James M Edie, ed, Carleton Dallery, trans, Evanston, IL: Northwestern University Press, 1964, p 1.

5 Coole, Diana, "The Inertia of Matter", in *New Materialisms—Ontology, Agency, and Politics*, Durham, NC: Duke University Press, 2010, p 94.

6 Leonard, Annie, *The Story of Stuff*, 2007 (online, www.storyofstuff.com), Braelan Murray, ed, cites Mocarelli et al: «Paternal concentrations of dioxin and sex ratio of offspring», *The Lancet*, 355 (9218) (2000), pp 1858–1863.

7 "From a Movie to a Movement", storyofstuff.org, accessed 21 April 2014.

8 Treib, "Simplicity and Belief", p 129.

In line with Ingold's thinking, I argue that objects should be raised to the status of *things*, that things should be designed to underline the connective and emergent flows inherent in materials, and that in the case of solar things these flows should be channelled into the perceptive processes of time, temperature and scale.

Typical effective solar objects, as opposed to affective solar things, are seen from without as purely functional. Robbed of the mystery of their sense experience, these objects are unaffected by time, obeying only laws of cause and effect. As Merleau-Ponty states, "Science only manipulates objects and renounces inhabiting them."[4] An example of a solar object is the cheap and widely available Charleston six-pack Solar Light. Function and price are the principal factors determining its manufacturing process, but the design fails to extend beyond basic functionalism or to activate a sense of time or temperature: day and night, they emit a constant pale blue light and are made of materials (crystalline panels, plastic and black pewter) that do not change over time. Although visually unobtrusive and useful, they therefore do not age well or adapt to their surroundings. Products such as this function as closed-loop systems whose materiality is reduced to physical and chemical processes, rather than as objects that promote sensuous experience and relate to their environment.[5]

The objects of today's material culture inevitably make their way into our immediate spheres, even for those of us who try to remain low-tech and minimal. Moreover, many techno objects that become quickly outdated are unrecyclable. In 2007, American proponent of sustainability Annie Leonard made a twenty-minute film about the life cycle of material goods. *The Story of Stuff* discusses the phenomenon of "planned obsolescence", the practice by which companies encourage frequent replacement of goods. For example, the computer manufacturer Macintosh create custom hardware for their goods designed to become rapidly obsolete, such as the charging plug for iPhone 7, which does not work for iPhone 8. When these millions of wires get incinerated, they produce dioxin, one of the most toxic manmade chemicals known.[6] According to Leonard, our society now consumes twice as much as it did fifty years ago. To help counteract this, she has established a community of 500,000 participants, which is working towards building a healthier planet and a "society based on better not more".[7]

If we accumulate too many objects, we lose the capacity to distinguish between objects and things. The architectural theorist Marc Treib describes how the few carefully selected things adorning a Japanese tearoom capture attention:

> Because the space *appeared* so simple, one looked more carefully, perhaps first noticing the beauty of the flower arrangement in the *tokonoma*, the appropriateness of the hanging painting to the current season, the texture of the mud plaster, the glaze of the tea bowl or the obscure light filtered thru one or more layers of rice paper.[8]

9 Ingold, "Bringing Things to Life", p 10.

10 Specifications of KS - S7070S: dimension (69.5 x
   69.5 x 3.2 mm); Pmax (0.192 W); Operating Voltage
   (3.5 V); Operating Current (55 mA); Open Circuit
   Voltage (4.8 V); Short Circuit Current (81 mA).
   Standard Test Conditions: Irradiance 1000 W/m2,
   AM 1.5, Module Temperature 25 degrees Celsius."
   China Solar Ltd Catalogue, China, 2013, p 13.

11 After extensive experimentation with chemical
   variation, some leaders in the LED industry now
   manage to expand the colour spectrum from
   cool white to warmer white. For example, electrical
   engineer Michael Edwards of Avioworks has
   sourced warm-toned LED bulbs from Germany
   (Avago Technologies).

12 An aspect of permanence is also expressed in the
   timeless shape of the material assembly, which
   forms a classic double cube shape, and also bears
   an element of cultural memory. The technological
   and sustainable nature of the photovoltaic
   material, on the other hand, signals novelty
   and a shared future.

As opposed to inert objects, lively things such as these give pleasure and enrich the experience of time spent in an interior. However, the problem that results from an excessive number of objects in our surroundings is not only lack of connection with materials but with the immaterial, such as the changing light passing over Japanese rice paper in the tearoom described above. If we replace the objects in our near spheres with things, they can become places freed from the 'noise' of objects, where we can connect with both the senses and, in the case of solar designs, with the immaterial forces that relate to sunlight—time, temperature, scale and energy. By channelling human perceptive processes, solar things can become affective; only then do they have the power to capture our attention.

One way in which the solar designs in Cocoon attempt to achieve the status of things is by using a type of photovoltaic material called amorphous thin film, which, when viewed from certain angles, functions as a mirror. Depending on viewing and sun angles, the PV panels either blend in with the designs' dark-red colour and faint stripes, or with the surroundings, by reflecting them in their mirrored surfaces. The panels connect with the sun both through their orientation and tilt, and through their regular illuminations that synchronise with solar rhythms. The technological elements of the lamp—electric board, inverter, batteries, wires, etc—thus merge with their biological aspects and become immersed in the 'circulations' of their environments.[9]

The amorphous thin film-type of photovoltaic panel performs better than the usual crystalline PV panel because even on rainy days the silicon solar cells will output a stable electric current,[10] though the panel does need to be bathed in daylight, either indoors or out, for eight hours a day to function. Solar lights also serve to lower electric bills, eliminate wires, illuminate automatically at dusk and offer multidirectional ambient light. Just as importantly, they can create affective indoor lighting by producing a 'warm' atmospheric glow. Thanks to research and development, LEDs, which typically give off a 'cold' bluish tone, can now emit a warmer-toned light.[11]

A further advantage of solar lighting is that it can open people's eyes to the cycles of the sun, by making visible a slower time rhythm of which we aren't usually aware. Cyclical time is expressed by reflecting routine functions, such as turning on lights with the fall of darkness, while the linear time of past and future can be illustrated by weathering and sustainability of the designs' organic and eco-tech surfaces. In addition, the designs' mirrored panels emphasise the present moment, by reflecting the ever-changing nature of the surrounding environment. Glass (including solar film-coated glass) is not subject to weathering like wood or stone and is not permanently affected by time unless it cracks. However, the thin film panels serve to contrast with the weathered surfaces of the lighting designs and signal the dialectics between permanence and novelty, as discussed in Chapter One.[12] Recycled or locally sourced biomaterials, such as seashells or reclaimed wood, refer to slow and local traditions of making and to cultural memory, while the high-tech

13 Solar Panel Specifications: diameter 100, max power (Pm) 0,86W, operating voltage (Vmp), 4V operating current (Imp); diameter 130, max power (Pm), 1,2W operating voltage (Vmp): 6V operating current (Imp).

14 Cook, Kim, "Biophilic Décor: Bring the Feel of Nature Indoors", *The Associated Press*, 13 December 2019.

15 Haverkamp, Michael, *Synesthetic Design – Handbook for a Multi-Sensory Approach*, Basel, Switzerland: Birkhauser, 2013.

materials of solar panels result from many stages of manufacturing carried out in different parts of the world, and have complex technical specifications.[13] Despite these contrasts, however, the distinction between technological and organic surfaces remains blurred.

This dichotomy between local and global is further reflected in the movements of the energy-collecting charts that accompany the solar things, s local conditions charted over time inform the global system. The energy production of solar panels can be read in quantitative recordings of their behaviour in different locations. An electrical engineer's data metre, for example, recording the output of a panel facing a window, reveals an abrupt downward swing when covered by a passing shadow. This change disrupts the regular pattern on which estimates for the panel's power output is based, thereby making the global universal system more local and specific: hence the term 'glocal'. At the same time, perceiving the change both visually and thermally, if one were to stand in front of the window where the PV panel was placed, reinforces intellectual understanding of the fact that the panel is producing less energy during its time in the shade.

Biophilia

The lighting and furniture in Cocoon House form part of a holistic environment, in which the products reflect the ideas represented by the architecture: as the house revolves around its natural setting, so do the biophilic products within it. The term 'biophilia', an affinity for the living world, was coined in the 1980s by American author and biologist E O Wilson,[14] who claimed that we have an instinctive drive to connect with nature, and that the more we connect the happier we are.

Biophilic design can bring the outdoors inside to spaces where it is most needed. As not every home can be flooded with daylight, plants and natural views the way Cocoon is, other attempts to bring the outside in may include features such as landscape paintings, floral wallpaper or potted plants. But by choosing products that use natural or eco materials, designers can introduce the benefits of biophilic design more effectively. The furniture pieces designed for Cocoon are all made of organic materials that evoke forms found in nature and could function as works of biophilia for any interior, though lighting designs have been customised. For example, algae and seashells that filter the bulbs of light fixtures signal the ocean nearby, an effect that is reinforced by incoming sea breezes and the sound of waves in the distance.[15]

—

I argue that the task of the designer is to underline the liveliness of solar things by enabling them to connect with people and their surroundings, through the manner in which they incorporate the photovoltaic material. As matter

16 See William E Connolly about the capacity
   of matter to self-organise, in Coole and Frost,
   "Materialities of Experience", p 179.

17 Ingold, "Bringing Things to Life", p 16.

18 Quote by Olafur Eliasson from his website,
   starbrick.info/en/research.html, accessed 14
   August 2013.

self-organises to a great extent,[16] the skill of the designer involves embracing the emergent characteristics of materials, which come alive by the way they reflect light and change colour over time in response to their environment. Lively things keep the metabolic systems of cities, gardens and homes going, and act as connective tissues rather than as self-contained objects. The solar lights are designed to connect in a similar animated and somewhat chaotic manner, as described by Tim Ingold:

> Modern society, of course, is averse to such chaos. Yet however much it has tried, through feats of engineering, to construct a material world that matches its expectations—that is, a world of discrete, well-ordered objects—its aspirations are thwarted by life's refusal to be contained. We might think that objects have outer surfaces, but wherever there are surfaces life depends on the continual exchange of materials across them. If, by 'surfacing' the earth or incarcerating bodies, we block that exchange, then nothing can live.[17]

The surfaces of the solar lights are designed to frame and direct natural and electric light in a way that enriches the experience of the space in which they are placed. By moving away from the realm of objects to things, and by awakening the senses of time, temperature and scale, these artefacts aim to lift us to the realm of affect and to initiate a more ethical relationship with the wider environmental context. The Danish–Icelandic artist Olafur Eliasson has expressed a similar view on the role of light in contemporary space:

> Light has a crucial impact on our understanding of our immediate surroundings, the larger geo-political context, sustainability, the consequences of our actions, the social relations in which we are entangled, as well as of ourselves. If we enhance our light sensibility, letting aesthetic and eco-ethical concerns intertwine, I think we will begin to conceive differently of space.[18]

By delivering different sensations of light in everyday environments, the solar lights described here attempt to do what Eliasson describes.

BIOPHILIC LIGHTING AND FURNITURE

Algae Lamp

These translucent cylindrical light shades are made from algae and cast a warm glow. After years of research, we found a formula for treating green marine algae (Chlorophyta) so it becomes firm and durable, yet malleable. The material retains its organic nature, translucency and colour when moulded, allowing each alga sheet to be handcrafted into a unique sculptural light shade with customisable shapes and finishes, including brass. Algae's colours are varied, rich and vibrant, and the individual units can be grouped in different ways to form chandeliers, or can function on their own as table lamps or sconces.

First dried and hand-moulded into basic shapes from everyday drinking glasses, the shades maintain their structural integrity when dry, but curl up along their bottom edges and therefore have many variations. While other designers have experimented with effects based on weaving, dying, pleating, gold-plating and embroidering, the design for Algae Lamp aims to expose the nature and beauty of the raw material. Algae carry associations with natural energy, an important theme in Cocoon House, and have the potential to be developed into an alternative to fossil fuel.[1] Grown in the right light and temperature conditions, they can be bioluminescent and absorb carbon emissions.

Our research has shown that an important way to make LED light appear warmer is to filter it through natural materials. Texture and shape are also factors: the unpredictable form of each shade after the drying/moulding process, along with its textured surface, help to softly dissipate the light, while brass or bronze fittings may also contribute to emitting a warmer light. As LED lighting technology improves, the material's colour range will widen; at the moment the range is narrow and the light therefore needs skilful filtering and dispersion. When backlit by electric light or sunlight, the algae resemble yellow glass, which may trigger a sense of temperature through colour perception.

Algae Lamp addresses sense of scale as well as senses of touch and temperature. The alga used derives from the waters of Peconic Bay, which is near Cocoon House. In an increasingly high-tech global world, local organic or biomaterials with known origins help connect people with the natural world.

[1] According to the head of Algal Biomass Organization, algae fuel could reach price parity with oil in a few years if granted tax credits. However, due to expensive development investments, algae fuel is actually more than 25 years away from commercial viability, wikipedia.com, accessed 28 October 2013.

Beanie Sofa

This comfortable textile-covered sofa, assembled in two parts, incorporates a pair of daybeds facing opposite directions. Its soft structure is filled with organic latex and lentil beans, which are malleable but support the natural curves and movements of the body, including the shapes required for good posture. In Cocoon, the daybeds are placed under skylights so users can view the sky.

Knotty Set

The Knotties is a set of indoor/outdoor armchairs made of natural rattan, comprising armchair, love seat and footrest. The name derives from the designs' sculptural knot forms, which are intended to give the user comfort and relaxation.

In Cocoon House, the Knotties are placed in the corners of the living room and bedrooms, which, according to Bachelard, who dedicated a whole chapter to corners in his *Poetics of Space*, are a significant position: "[T]he corner is a haven that ensures us one of the things we prize most highly—immobility. The corner is a sort of half-box, part walls, part door. It will serve as an illustration for the dialectics of inside and outside."[1]

1 Bachelard, *The Poetics of Space*, p 137.

Cantilever Table

Shaped like an ocean wave, this versatile, extended, C-shaped side table with cantilevered top can be made of recycled polished stainless steel, brass or transparent Lucite. Its top surface projects at sofa height from a solid base which appears as if held down by screws. The polished version of the table is inspired by the duality of solidity and fluidity and conveys a sense of liquidity through the light reflections captured in its curving surface, which in turn echoes the curved walls of the house. The reflective top can be placed so as to mirror specific views of the surroundings, or to amplify indoor light features such as candles.

Crystallised Set

Like crystals, the different facets of the Crystallised Table and Chair catch and reflect the changing light. Similar to organic crystal formations, the surfaces of the indoor/outdoor hexagonal table and chair are bent at 120-degree and 150-degree angles, respectively. The table contains insets with three removable serving trays and is available in two sizes—smaller cocktail and larger dining table. The chair is also made in two sizes—children and adults.

The dining set resembles origami, which suits the manufacturing process of bent metal or wood. It is available in a variety of finishes and comes in separate parts for ease of shipping.

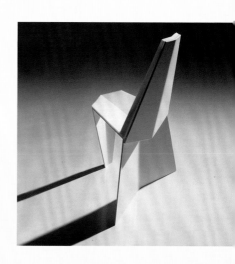

"Materials can po
energy as well a
indexes, scents
temperature grad
plant physiology-
generate co

ntially transform
alter humidity
uminosity levels,
nts, air masses and
n other words, they
tant novelty."

Cape Chair

Cape Chair is inspired by the organic forms found in ice and snowscapes in Norway. The design takes its name from the chair's double-curved, cape-like back, which is countered by a single front leg. The prototype was fabricated by an engineer from the Norwegian oil industry who specialised in double-curved industrial parts.

Outdoor Twist Sofa

Inspired by natural forms in Arctic nature, such as melting ice and intertwining tree trunks, Outdoor Twist Sofa is a customisable, modular, outdoor L-shaped rattan sofa with integrated daybed. Comfortable, lightweight and easy to transport, it is assembled from three parts. Unlike a conventional sofa, however, Twist Sofa is designed with sloping, soft surfaces to accommodate different lounging positions and encourage social intimacy.

Vanity Table

Inspired by melting snow and icicles, this small, lightweight and versatile vanity table fits easily into most bedrooms or entry spaces. The shiny, multipurpose table surface incorporates a bowl for cosmetics or keys, and can also hold water for floating candles/flowers, or function as a small desk.

Bird Bed and Chair

Inspired by birds in flight, Bird Bed and Bird Chair are designed to resemble the profiles of flying birds while also fitting the human body. Bird Chair has one wing raised to serve as a backrest, while Bird Bed has both wings flat to provide a daybed. Both can accommodate up to two people on a single narrow spine or foot and are crafted from recycled aluminium that adapts gently to the body. At Cocoon, these pieces act as focal points in the garden to entice inhabitants outside when weather permits.

SOLAR THINGS

Latitude Lamp

Latitude Lamp, an indoor/outdoor solar powered light that emits ambient illumination, consists of a basic module of interlocking cubes whose dimensions are based on the square format of its amorphous thin-film solar panel. As a global product customised for specific locations and fabricated in a range of materials and sizes, including a mini 3D-printed version,[1] the lamp's geometry can be automatically registered in a digital file and then 3D printed so that its shape and the tilt of its solar panel are optimised according to latitude. However, it is designed for annual solar power collection only, rather than for tracking the sun's path from moment to moment, as the tracking option was eliminated early in the design process due to budget. The lamp acts as an iconic visual signifier of geographic location, and serves to arouse perception by addressing the senses of time, temperature, scale and material.

Latitude Lamp can function on its own as a freestanding sculpture, or can be assembled into a variety of daylight-modulating screens that filter daylight through perforations. These perforations project moving diamond patterns onto floors and walls and awaken awareness of the sun's cycles, while temperature can be experienced either through the shading provided by the screens, or indirectly through colour perception of the LEDs, which modulate light. Moreover, as amorphous thin film functions efficiently with indirect light, the lamp does not need to face strictly south and turns on automatically at fall of darkness.

The shape of the lamp, formed by two interlocking cubes, evolves in response to intrinsic and extrinsic forces.[2] Weighed down by the technical elements (batteries, inverter, wires, etc), the base provides stability, while the upper cube is designed to tilt perpendicular to the sun's rays. At the same time, the materials of the lamp incorporate a sense of time. The recycled metal version, for example, carries with it the visible history of the manual sanding of its planes, of scratches and scrapes, as well as its invisible history of having been recycled from a past

1   Latitude Lamp made its debut in the Shadow and Light group exhibition in Løvestad, Sweden, in July 2010. The following year, three versions of Latitude Lamp were published and exhibited at the Global Design New York University exhibitions and symposiums, in Manhattan in 2011/2018 at the NYU Gallatin School, and in London at The Building Centre in 2012. The 3D-printed versions of the lamp, accompanied by a computer screen for online customisation and orders, were exhibited in Manhattan at the Digital Forming stand at the 3D Print Show in February 2014, and at the ICFF (International Contemporary Furniture Fair) with the New Lab group exhibition stand in May 2014.

2   Inspired by British industrial designer Ross Lovegrove's notion of 'organic essentialism': "I believe that if I spend the time to study the earth, evolution and time, it will give me something that is organic, biological and where form grows where you need it." Ross Lovegrove at Phillips de Pury, 26 March 2007, Ross Lovegrove, British Council, Design Museum—Industrial/ Product Designer, 1958—Design Museum Collection, dezeen online design magazine, accessed 12 October 2009.

3 It was thought that translucent algae and snakeskin would blend with the PV panel's rusty colour and transmit an orange glow (given the lights were placed inside the lamp), but both failed.

4 The skins are tanned using hydroelectric power and thermal water, then hand-strung in a small cottage/factory near the Arctic Circle. arctic-designs.com, accessed 7 November 2013.

5 Milgo/Bufkin have been combining state-of-the-art technology and old-world craftsmanship since 1916. In 1996, they started their research branch, Algorythms, in conjunction with Pratt Institute, to develop cutting-edge design techniques using CAD software, giant press breaks and metal shears.

existence. Over time, whichever material is used (which can range from COR-TEN steel to translucent plastic, wood grain and even salmon skin) also gradually acquires the marks of external forces such as rain, oxidation and fingerprints, which in turn renders them more tactile. Thermal and atmospheric sensations can be created through the light of bulbs that emit a warm glow similar to candlelight, while the steel version acts as a reflector of the light effects that surround it.

To obtain as warm a light as possible, a variety of LED bulbs and materials that play with light were tested.[3] At the same time, four prototypes were fabricated in three materials: salmon skin, reclaimed wood and recycled steel. The wooden version was found to emit a more yellow colour than the steel, whereas the translucent 3D-printed lamp produced a stronger glow because the LED bulb inside its body bounced off its translucent white surfaces.

Latitude Lamp also addresses the sense of scale by operating at, and connecting with, different distances. In terms of its own scale, it can function as a house, pavilion, garden lantern, modular screen or table lamp; through its tilt, it connects with the movement of the sun (as the result of mass customisation) and with a specific locality; and at a more immediate scale, its surfaces and textures appeal to the body's sense of touch. Awareness of the immediate vicinity can also be awoken by arousing a sense of place, by responding to the location's seasonal cycles, and by reflecting local scenery. For example, a lamp placed in Long Island, New York, displays a tilt of 45 degrees and mirrors local flora. In Tjøme, Norway, the panel tilts at 60 degrees and reflects views of the cliffs and fast-moving clouds typical of the area. In addition, the Norwegian lamp is made of salmon skin because of the local associations of the material. Sometimes referred to as 'Arctic leather',[4] salmon skin is usually discarded after a fishing haul. In Brooklyn, New York, local metal fabricators Milgo/Bufkin fabricated the first prototype of the New York lamp from recycled steel railway scraps.[5] Hence, while global solar technology determines the PV panel's materiality and function, local context informs the materials of the base; together, they emphasise the lamp's essentially 'glocal' nature. Mostafavi and Leatherbarrow have discussed how rusted steel reflects local climate and conditions.

BASE

FACE

join BASE and FACE

put BASE over FACE   insert end of FACE into pockets   UNIT A

BASE

fold in half   unfold

FACE

join BASE and FACE

put BASE over FACE   insert end of FACE into pockets   UNIT B

ASSEMBLY METHOD

assemble 3 units   fold both sides upward with FACE on bottom

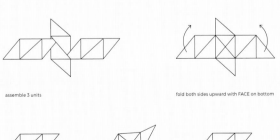

3 × UNIT A   3 × UNIT B   3 × UNIT A

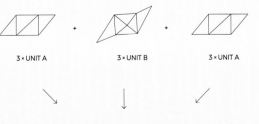

Mass customisation of the mini 3D-printed version of Latitude Lamp (w 11.1 × d 13.1 × h 14.8 cm/w 4.4 × d 5.2 × h 5.8 in), made from recycled coloured plastic powder, enables it to be manufactured in a variety of materials and colours, depending on individual environments and preferences.[7] When ordering a lamp, customers can select their preferred material and colour, and digitally enter their location's latitude (from 0 to 70) on a slider to adjust the lamp's tilt. In its ability to oscillate between the global and the personal, the mini-lamp shares characteristics with other customised, mass-produced products such as the iPod or iPhone, as Antoine Picon has described:

> Emblematic of today's digital lifestyles, the Apple iPod also produces a good illustration of the recurring duality between standardization and uniqueness. On the one hand, the development of the player is linked to a massive commercial enterprise that delivers preformatted music to millions of customers. On the other hand, the same music, as soon as it is stored on a teenager's player, becomes 'his' music.[8]

The most lightweight version of the lamp is made of 1 mm-thick material, as light as paper and as thin as eggshell, but it is also durable, flexing slightly when squeezed. This mini version can be held in the hand and pointed at the sun, thus bringing touch, technology and the sun together in an accessible manner and making the holder more conscious of their geographic location.

The original prototype for Latitude Lamp (see drawing on page 59) was made of origami paper, an organic translucent material that glows when backlit, and had its panel tilted at 45 degrees for solar collection in New York City. However, it could function anywhere in the world by adjusting its shape parametrically according to latitude. The drawing illustrates what happens to the cubes when they are placed in a range of contexts around the globe and manipulated for optimal power collection.[9] However, just as important as the solar panel's location and angle is the provenance of the lamp's material. Organic substances such as salmon skin, for example, can often be understood more easily than manufactured materials, and provide reassurance and familiarity. As Robert Kronenburg asserts:

> Recognizably natural materials have a presence based on human experience that is tested, safe and sure. They have a realness, a grounding in the world, which is recognizable and identifiable. They have a rapport with human beings because we believe, even if this is not always true, that we can identify their source.[10]

7   By Dr Siavash Mahdavi, Riccardo Bovo and other partners at Digital Forming and withinlab.

8   Picon, *Digital Culture in Architecture*, p 51.

9   The Norwegian architect Christian Norberg-Schulz called this type of deformation 'topology', a term meaning the study of objects that retain their properties when they change shape, such as by stretching or tilting. Christian Norberg-Schulz, *Intentions in Architecture*, Cambridge, MA: MIT Press, 1965, pp 43–45.

10 Kronenburg, Robert, *Spirit of the Machine—Technology as an Inspiration in Architectural Design*, UK: Wiley-Academy, 2001, p 62.

11 For the wooden lamp for New York, I walked up a
flight of stairs to the roof of my studio in Brooklyn
to reclaim a piece of discarded wood.

A lamp's geographic location may therefore be conveyed more effectively by its
materials than by its relation to the sun. For example, three different lamps were
fabricated for Dubai, New York and Norway, all using local, recycled materials:
rusted steel, wood and salmon skin, respectively.[11] In each case, the intention was
that the material used would be tied to its location and convey a sense of place.

By becoming fully integrated into its chosen environment, Latitude Lamp
can therefore stimulate the senses of time, temperature, scale and material that
will enable it to become affective on a personal level. It is only through acquiring
desirability that solar lights can succeed in the global marketplace and address
the fact that, despite their low cost and availability, they have not, as yet, been
widely embraced.

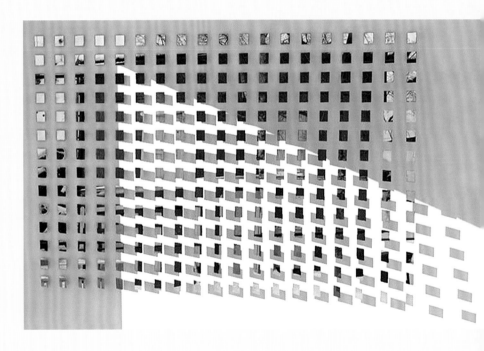

Sun Calendar

Consisting of a rectangular grid of amorphous thin-film PV panels, the wall
hanging resembles a typical monthly wall calendar divided into squares. At the
same time, the mirrored surface creates a pixelated reflection of its surroundings,
producing a slow-moving sequence of sunlight and shadow patterns. A series of
sun studies carried out at different times of the day and year determined the
overall shape of the screen, which needed several iterations to ensure size and
spacing of the pixels were conducive to forming an apprehensible image.

The diurnal and seasonal schedule of sun diagrams reflected by the screen
operates according to both cyclical and linear notions of time, reinforced by the
waking and sleeping rituals that take place in the bedroom corridor where the
screen hangs.[1] The corridor is fronted by a heat-collecting east-facing glass façade,
which promotes bodily warmth during the day, especially the morning hours. This
experience is reinforced by colour perception at night, when LED bulbs emit a

1 The panels have to be attached to the wall by
acrylic rods that tilt at precise angles to produce
this effect.

2   Volf's work focuses on the seasons and geographical orientation, with the room as a creator of light. His film, "Light, Architecture and Health" (2013), about circadian rhythms, is a 30-minute time lapse of seasons and orientations throughout the day and year in different corners of the world. The film was an educational project of the School of Architecture Aarhus based on Carlo Volf's PhD dissertation, and focused on the health-related significance of light in architecture.

3   The aedicule and its connection with memory in the work of Charles Moore is discussed by Jorge Otero-Pailos in *Architecture's Historical Turn— Phenomenology and the Rise of the Postmodern*, Minneapolis, MN: University of Minnesota Press, 2010, p xxix.

4   Moore's PhD dissertation from Princeton, from where he graduated in 1957, entitled "Water and Architecture", was inspired by Gaston Bachelard's writings on the four elements, and, according to Otero-Pailos, was "the first analysis of Gaston Bachelard's work within American architectural discourse. In it, Moore developed the notion that all architecture originated in archetypal psychological experiences, which he called "poetic images". Ibid, p xxvii.

5   Bachelard, *The Poetics of Space*, p 60.

6   Moore and Bloomer, *Body, Memory, and Architecture*.

warm-toned light that is reflected on the wall behind them. By creating warmth, both literally and metaphorically, this corridor of the house therefore nurtures biological cycles that occur at specific times of the day and year, as well as perception of time. Moreover, as the PV screen operates according to the slow passage of the sun, it engages the mind in a more restful perceptive process, allowing it to connect with nature's clock and strengthening awareness of natural light patterns.

However, the calendar also refers to time cycles metaphorically as well as literally, by reflecting the image of a traditional nineteenth-century carriage house across the garden. Situated on an inherited compound property, the carriage house is now inhabited by the owner's brother and family, and holds personal memories for the owner who spent much of her childhood there. These memories are therefore stimulated by the reflections, but, because of the fragmentary effect of the pixilation, the house appears ghostly, blurring the distinction between real and unreal, and between past and present time.

One of the inspirations for the calendar was a study by Danish architect Carlo Volf, of moving light and sun patches entering four cardinally oriented rooms in Denmark, where he demonstrated that our body responds to the rotation of the sun (when the sun is in the north, we are at midnight).[2] If, for example, a west-facing window were replaced by an east-facing one, inhabitants would receive the benefits of direct morning sun, which would set in motion circadian rhythms more effectively; on the other hand, the pleasure of the evening sun would be lost. His work brings up the question of how Sun Calendar would function on a wall with a different orientation, as well as in different locations, as this would alter both its geometry and play of light across the surface.

In order to understand how the screen might function as a 'glocal' product, three prototypes were produced based on solar data in three cities: Oslo, New York and Dubai. Placed at a 90-degree angle to a same-sized window, the three screens were roughly the same shape with slight variations, though a northern climate was found to be the most suitable environment, as the sun in the northern hemisphere is lower in the sky and therefore reaches farther into the room and higher up the wall. Lack of sunlight hitting the screen in wintertime proved to be problematic in all three locations: to guarantee global viability, the work must be placed next to, or in front of, a large, high window.

The concept of memory in the design of the bedroom corridor of the house was partly inspired by the 'aedicule',[3] developed by American architect and writer Charles Moore. An aedicule is a small semi-enclosed space within the larger area of the home. Wherever it was built, by setting the stage for bodily stimulation, Moore's aedicule grounded human memories in that particular place. Moore's mentor, Gaston Bachelard, about whom he wrote his doctoral dissertation,[4] writes of the eye, the body and the other senses collaborating to awaken memories of a room: " [...] well beyond any geometry that can be drawn, we must recapture the quality of the light; then come the sweet smells that linger in the empty rooms, setting an aerial seal on each room in the house of memory."[5] In *Body, Memory, and Architecture*,[6] co-authored with Kent Bloomer, Moore, too, advocates concrete bodily experiences and place-bound memories, while distinguishing between the abstractions of history and the more experiential notion of memory. By underlining the sensual experience of sunlight combined with childhood memories of the house across the lawn, Sun Calendar brings together an embodied notion of memory with a more abstract and mental one.

As well as the senses of time and temperature, Sun Calendar underlines sense of scale, as the corridor surrounding it sets the stage for experiences that are expansive as well as grounded in domestic routines, in ways that are reminiscent of a Charles Moore aedicule. In a Moore aedicule, one of the four elements (earth, air, fire, water), or a combination of them, serves to anchor and arouse the "material imagination",[7] by bringing architecture into intimate sensual contact with the body. In a similar way, the screen captures water reflections that bounce off the cistern a few feet away, which, together with the presence of sunlight in Cocoon House, stimulate the material imagination and encourage the mind to wander outside the confines of the house.

A further inspiration on the mirrored PV panels in Sun Calendar was the work of artist Robert Smithson, particularly his use of mirrors to explore the environment. His indoor piece, *Leaning Mirror* (1969), for example, was placed by a window to reflect the surrounding sky and light, and relates to the Yucatan mirror earthworks from the same year for which he stuck mirrors into the ground:

> I picked a place and then stuck the mirrors directly into the ground so that they reflected the sky. I was dealing with actual light as opposed to paint. I was interested in capturing the actual light on each spot, bringing it down to the ground.[8]

Smithson, however, downplayed his own agency, suggesting that the mirrors caught the light in an incidental fashion, as though light merely befell them.[9] The mirrors in Sun Calendar, on the other hand, are placed intentionally, to capture a particular reflection and to optimise solar power collection. Sun Calendar also borrows from the sense of primordial grandeur expressed in Smithson's Yucatan works, but represents an essentially activist attitude to the environment, in contrast with the more passive one implicit in Smithson's mirrors, which signal no future for technology. These two divergent eco-political philosophies are telling of the circumstances of the times in which they were created: Smithson's radical political philosophy, informed by entropic theory, found apparent confirmation in the global political crises of the late 60s, while Sun Calendar is born from the age of global warming, and represents twenty-first century eco-ethics and techno-optimism.

The pixelated screen of Sun Calendar also addresses the tendency of the digital age to counteract apprehension of a wider sense of time. The calendar's emphasis on the sun's movements is a way of telling time that is rhythmic rather than disjointed. As opposed to the tendency of digital screen to create a feeling of being trapped in the fragmented now, Sun Calendar encourages reflection upon past and future, while underlining the focused energy of the sun and its slow rhythms. The wall hanging is thus conceived as a device for expanding the small moments that take place in the corridor into a larger time perspective.

7   "The material imagination [...] aims at producing that which, in being, is both primitive and eternal." Bachelard, *The Poetics of Space*, p xiii.

8   Robert Smithson quoted by Ron Graziani, in *Robert Smithson and the American Landscape*, Cambridge, UK: Cambridge University Press, 2004 (113), p 46.

9   Roberts, Jennifer L, *Mirror Travels—Robert Smithson and History*, New Haven, CT, and London, UK: Yale University Press, 2004, p 103.

Solar Chandelier

Constructed from translucent seashells and photovoltaic modules, Solar Chandelier belongs to the collection of solar things described here that is especially for Cocoon and is fabricated in our studio and workshop at New Lab, in Brooklyn Navy Yard. Pieces such as this aim to demystify PV technology by exposing their components—PCB, battery, wires, LED, etc—in a legible manner to make them more approachable.

Hung in front of a window, the chandelier functions as a type of solar clock, its photovoltaic modules powering LED bulbs that activate automatically at dusk to illuminate a variety of translucent materials (seashells or other organic matter) and to highlight hourly and seasonal solar rhythms. When active, the chandeliers offer a warm, multidirectional ambient light while also casting patterns onto surrounding surfaces. Passing breezes make it a wind chime, too; in the setting of Cocoon, the sound of the sea breeze signals the ocean nearby. The glass amorphous thin film panels, when viewed from certain angles, mirror the view out of the window they face. The visual and acoustic aspects of the reflective thin-film material therefore serve to connect the interior and exterior environments. Like the other solar things in Cocoon, Solar Chandelier explores solar cells as perceptual devices for mediating light.

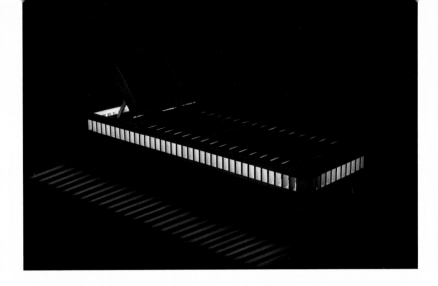

Solar Lounger

nea studio developed Solar Lounger to fulfil both seating and lighting functions outdoors.[1] A wooden slatted lounger, the work contains an integral mirrored photovoltaic panel situated in the adjustable backrest, which reflects the surroundings and collects power to illuminate lights inside its main body at dusk.[2]

Solar Lounger can also register local climate conditions, including temperature, humidity, wind or sunlight levels, through the use of embedded sensors, which feed information back into the system as data. In summer and winter, it lights up red or blue to signal hot and cold, these colours turning brightest when temperatures are at their most extreme. The photovoltaic panels belong to a breed of new materials, referred to by American architect Sheila Kennedy as "soft infrastructure",[3] which operate like an "instrument" by engaging dynamically with their environment:[4] "Those materials are creating a different definition of infrastructure. We used to think of infrastructure as a technology, or a physical object, but now materials can actually produce infrastructural effects—creating energy, creating light and storing power."[5] Unlike 'hard', centralised power plants fuelled by oil, gas, coal or uranium, Solar Lounger therefore exemplifies a form of decentralised, renewable technology that conserves energy and follows 'soft energy paths', a term coined by American physicist and environmental scientist Amory Lovins in 1976.[6]

1   With architect Raphael Walther and electrical engineer Michael Edwards from Avioworks.

2   The energy from the solar panel is stored in a 12-amp/hour battery during the day, and lights strips of electroluminescent tape at night.

3   Another example of soft infrastructure is Mitchell Joachim's Lamb Car, whose soft surfaces are made of layers of low pressure ETFE pillows. Joachim has described how "padded cars hail a crunch-free future". These small solar-powered vehicles can dynamically change the grid, herding around the hard-edged, oil-consuming hummer trucks and gently nudging them off the streets. From Mitchell Joachim's Ted Talk, "City 2.0", TedxBerlin, 2013.

4   Mitchell Joachim: "Maybe it's more like an instrument that is played differently based on what the music calls for." Louise Harpman, Mitchell Joachim, and Peder Anker, "nea studio", *Global Design: Elsewhere Envisioned*, Munich, Germany: Prestel Publishing, 2014, p 85.

5   Kennedy is quoted from an interview with Rob Goodier, "Portable Light's solar textiles generate mobile power off the grid", 26 July 2012, in Engineeringforchange.org, accessed 16 October 2013.

6   In "Energy Strategy: The Road Not Taken", 1976, an article for *Foreign Affairs Journal*, Amory Lovins coined the term 'soft energy paths'. Robert Bradley Jr, "Remembering the Birth of Conservatism, Part II: Amory Lovins' 'Soft Energy Path'", 3 May 2011, mastersource.org, accessed 20 December 2013.

Chapter Three
ARCHITECTURE

Introduction

1   Specialists are more likely to be involved in the later design phases, both in small and large projects. See Jouri Kanters, Miljana Horvat, and Marie-Claude Dubois, "Tools and Methods Used by Architects for Solar Design," *Energy and Buildings* 68, 2014, p 724.

2   evelectricity.com/solar/solar-neighborhood.php, accessed 30 July 2014.

3   "6 disadvantages of solar energy", *Solar Panels Photovoltaic*, December 2013, solarpanelsphotovoltaic.net/disadvantages-of-solar-energy/, accessed 30 July 2014.

4   *The Economist* cited a report from Bloomberg New Energy Finance, 16 March 2012, via Forbes, that found that "technological advancements, process improvements, and changes in the structure of the industry suggest that further price reductions are likely to occur in coming years". *The Economist*, 28 December 2012.

5   The design of Solar Umbrella House integrates a floating milky-coloured canopy or umbrella into its light, planar architectural language meant for California indoor/outdoor living. Soft House boasts a sail-like light-modulating PV façade of white textile that suits its marine island setting.

In current architectural design, solar energy tends to be discussed in technical terms. However, in order for photovoltaic panels to become fully accepted as a building material they must be designed according to a wider range of parameters than just cost and energy efficiency: architects should be able to investigate solar cells not only as tools for collecting power, but also as perceptual devices for mediating sunlight into designed spaces.

Although countless examples of photovoltaic systems added onto buildings populate our built landscape today, architects rarely incorporate them into their designs at the beginning of the design process,[1] mainly because of the still-prevailing notion that they are purely technical elements. The internet is full of comments such as: "Some homeowners say no to solar because they don't want an ugly array jimmy rigged to their roof. I can't say I blame them as we put a lot of money into keeping our property looking good."[2] Another website about PV panels quotes: "With solar power, your roof will have these black misplaced squares upon it."[3]

As the solar industry continues to improve in aesthetic options and prices,[4] architects have, however, begun to integrate solar technologies as design elements. Some works of architecture that integrate photovoltaics include Solar Umbrella House by Brooks and Scarpa, 2005, surmounted by an airy PV canopy/umbrella, and Soft House by Kennedy & Violich (KVA Matx), 2013, adorned by a rotating solar textile façade.[5] Two other examples are Garcia and Montiel of QVE Arquitectos, who added coloured, semi-transparent PV skylights to the San Anton market in Madrid, and Rintala Eggertsson Architects, who

6 San Anton's Market renovation imitates nineteenth-century British industrial construction style, and has a 168-sq m skylight made of photovoltaic glazing units fully integrated into the building. Cabinet House, which forms part of the MAXXI Museum by Zaha Hadid, is a wooden construction formed as a set of large steps, with a PV façade and roof. The house is designed to receive rain and sunshine from above and to use these elements to create atmosphere and energy.

7 In an initiative called IEA-SCH Task 41, "Solar Energy and Architecture", which analysed barriers, needs and strategies surrounding tools and methods used by architects in solar design (http://solarintegration solutions.org/). Maria Cristina Munari Probst, Christian Roecker, "Criteria for Architectural Integration of Active Solar Systems," Ecole Polytechnique Fédérale de Lausanne (EPFL), Switzerland, IEA Task 41, Subtask A, Energy Procedia 30, 2012, SciVerse Science Direct, Elsevier Ltd, pp 1195–1204.

8 International Energy Agency, 2011 (executive summary only), full version via George Washington University's Solar Institute, at mediamatters.org/research/2013/01/24/myths-and-facts-about-solar-energy/192364, accessed 13 June 2013.

9 Dr Marie-Claude Dubois and Jouri Kanters, from Lund University, Sweden, and Miljana Horvat, from Ryerson University, Ontario, also researched this issue as part of the Task 41 initiative, and recommended that BPS (Building Performance Simulation) tools be user-friendlier and less expensive: "Future BPS tools should work as design tools, being able to support comparisons between competing design alternatives in relation to energy use and production." Jouri Kanters, et al, "Tool and Methods Used by Architects for Solar Design," p 728.

10 Parametric design is a process based on algorithmic thinking that enables the expression of parameters and rules that, together, define, encode and clarify the relationship between design intent and response.

designed Cabinet House as part of the MAXXI museum in Rome,[6] with PV solar windows. Architect and solar energy analyst Maria Cristina Munari Probst has also made significant progress in researching the architectural integration of photovoltaics, and developed a website allowing architects to access innovative solar products.[7] But despite these advances, progress still needs to be made if the solar industry is to emerge from its status as a niche market, and more architects are to consider photovoltaic panels as design materials.[8] In particular, there is a requirement for skill and tool development amongst architects to implement these technologies, and better communication is needed to convince clients of the validity of the solar option.[9] Government also plays a central role by providing tax incentives; while in Germany roofs are replete with PV arrays due to robust financial incentives, in certain locations like the state of Arizona whose southern climate would benefit from solar power, there are few.

This chapter explores how emerging environmental strategies and technologies, such as the architectural integration of photovoltaic systems, can be designed as integral elements to enrich our experience of architecture and daylight, and how these have been applied in Cocoon House.

Just as I distinguished between solar "objects" and "things" in the previous chapter, here I will differentiate between solar "buildings" and "architecture". Effective solar buildings, as opposed to *affective* solar architecture, favour quantitative standards of environmental performance over qualitative experience. For example, Passive House-certified buildings and parametric digital coding,[10] although efficient in their potential optimisation of environmental technologies, have a tendency to focus on technology at the expense of design.[11] Also, a

11 Passive House presentation of Artist's Studio, Bill
Ryall Architects, Orient Point, 2012, by David White
engineer, Right Environments, 19 February 2013,
at Trespa, 62 Greene St., New York, NY. During the
one hour-long presentation, there was not a
single mention of architecture.

12 LEED, established in 2000 by the US Green
Building Council, provides a checklist of points,
from water efficiency to sustainable materials and
passive/active solar power collection.

13 https://living-future.org/lbc/?gclid=Cj0KCQiAhs79
BRDOARIsAC6XpaX-AITq_n1gYvTEjXBG8ErAClgXS
4ikVomQGywtgqHGYJL1-UpzDS0aAmJ9EALw_
wcB, accessed 17 November 2020.

14 Typical programs include Rhino, Grasshopper,
Revit, Sketch-Up, Ecotect, eQuest and Tas.

15 Court, Brian, "Case Study: Cascadia Center for
Sustainable Design and Construction, Seattle,
Washington", design firm The Miller Hull Partnership,
client the Bullitt Foundation, Onsite Energy Systems,
in François Lévy, *BIM—In Small-Scale Sustainable
Design*, Hoboken, NJ: John Wiley and Sons, 2012,
p 202.

preoccupation with conforming to technical criteria, such as those set out by ASHRAE (American Society of Heating, Refrigerating and Air-Conditioning Engineers), often results in predictable environments characterised by uniform material palettes, lighting and thermal conditions. In striving to meet LEED (Leadership in Energy and Environmental Design) or other environmental standards of excellence,[12] architects therefore often sacrifice design in favour of technology, particularly with the growing pressure for solar buildings to satisfy technological requirements.

One example of a solar building in which architectural design gets lost in the pursuit of standards of sustainability is the Cascadia Center for Sustainable Design and Construction by the Miller Hull Partnership, in Seattle, Washington. Here, stringent standards of environmental performance are the overriding consideration and the architects have leant heavily on technology to meet the energy requirements of the Living Building Challenge, one of the more ambitious green building standards.[13]

According to Miller Hull, the main struggle during the design process was to balance daylight requirements with the size and geometry of the vast photovoltaic array determined by parametric digital design programs.[14] Although the use of such programs can give form to energy, they can only handle a few parameters at a time, making it difficult for architects to adapt them to real-life situations where more parameters may be at play.

The fact that the architects and engineers did not focus on the sensory aspects of sunlight in their design for the Cascadia Center is apparent in the way the building is documented in the book *BIM—In Small-Scale Sustainable Design*, where it is depicted from a purely exterior perspective.[15] Hence the architects and author have neglected to detail the material and lighting conditions inside the building, and have not recorded the potential of the building skin to mediate sunlight affectively in terms of reflection, opacity and transparency.

"Emerging enviro
and technol
architectural integr
systems, can be d
elements to enric
architecture

nental strategies

ies, such as the

on of photovoltaic

igned as integral

our experience of

and daylight."

"The key question is not how
sustainable architecture and design
can improve the environment, but
how they can initiate a dialogue
between humans and the planet."

The building's main feature is a dominating solar array, which envelops the roof and most of the southern façade. Because the solar apparatus covers so much of the building's outer surface (about two-thirds), it appears alienating, overly shiny, loud and self-referential, as opposed to osmotic. American literary critic and political theorist Fredric Jameson has criticised another building, the Westin Bonaventure Hotel in Los Angeles,[16] for its similarly copious and overbearing number of reflective surfaces. Here, mirrored glass does not allow the gaze to pass through as the building aspires to be an enclosed world:

> [...] the glass skin achieves a peculiar and placeless dissociation of the Bonaventure from its neighborhood: it is not even an exterior, inasmuch as when you seek to look at the hotel's outer walls you cannot see the hotel itself but only the distorted images of everything that surrounds it.[17]

16 Designed by John Portman in 1976.

17 Jameson, Fredric, *Postmodernism, Or, the Cultural Logic of Late Capitalism*, Durham, NC: Duke University Press, 1991, p 42.

18 Court, "Case Study: Cascadia Center for Sustainable Design and Construction", pp 200–203.

19 Examples of such solar buildings can be found in Othmar Humm and Peter Toggweiler, *Photovoltaics in Architecture—The Integration of Photovoltaic Cells in Building Envelopes*, Basel, Switzerland: Birkhauser, 1993, pp 62–63.

20 Pallasmaa, *The Eyes of the Skin*, pp 63–64.

21 "National building standards—as defined by ASHRAE regulation 55-2004—require that 80% of all building occupants exposed to the same conditions within a space must be 'comfortable' at any time." Jenny Lovell, *Building Environments— An Integrated Approach*, New York, NY: Princeton Architectural Press, 2010, pp 19–20.

22 Heschong, *Thermal Delight in Architecture*, taken from the title of her book.

Like the Bonaventure, the Cascadia Center's overbearing reflective surfaces prevent interaction with the outside world, detaching it from human and local scales, although, unlike the Bonaventure, it allows passers-by to see through windows at eye level. The energy requirements for this building, set out by the Living Building Challenge, included net-zero energy and water expenditure, a set of standards so stringent that the architects had to ask to raise the building another storey in order to meet them. As a result, the surrounding buildings do not receive the level of sunlight required by code,[18] and minimal internal allowances of sunlight were sacrificed for the sake of solar power production.

Like the Cascadia Center, many contemporary sustainable buildings are technologically determined and revolve around their own self-enclosed systems.[19] Solar buildings like these reveal few perceptible aspects of time, such as the ageing of materials or passing of the solar clock, and fail to focus on experience in time duration. Pallasmaa describes this tendency: "A building is not an end in itself [...]. Architectural space is lived space rather than physical space, and lived space always transcends geometry and measurability."[20] Equally, in their strict adherence to standards such as those imposed by ASHRAE,[21] solar buildings sometimes miss the opportunity to address sense of temperature in such a way as to create thermal pleasure, or "thermal delight", to borrow American architect Lisa Heschong's term.[22] Driven primarily by numeric parameters, including the attainment of an unchanging thermal environment, they also often omit to integrate heating, ventilation and

23 Ibid, p 17.

24 Lovell, *Building Environments*, pp 19–20.

air-conditioning (HVAC) systems into the design. By contrast, Heschong recommends a non-holistic approach towards the thermal sense, to counter the prevailing assumption that one thermal standard suits everyone and every environment: "The use of all our extremely sophisticated environmental control systems is directed to this one end—to produce standard comfort zone conditions."[23] However, human comfort is more complex than it is made out to be by officially accepted temperature and humidity levels. As American architect and author Jenny Lovell explains:

> [...] it is generally accepted that an internal temperature range of 68–78 degrees F, at 30–70% humidity, is a reasonable comfort zone for people against which building environmental systems can be measured. However, comfort is both more complex and more subtle than quantitative measures of temperature and relative humidity, and we are not limited to these ranges. Thermal comfort alone is defined by dynamic spatial conditions of internal and external temperature, humidity levels, and air velocity, together with factors related directly to an individual: clothing type, activity level, age, gender, health condition, metabolic rate, perception, and memory.[24]

25 "Happily, we're seeing an increasing number
of architects and engineers paying attention to
the cry of occupants for operable windows in
non-residential buildings. Unfortunately, they
are often limited in their flexibility to pursue such
options because of the relatively narrow range
of interior thermal environments allowed by
ASHRAE Standard 55, and assumed to be
universally applicable across all building types,
climates, and populations." G S Brager and R de
Dear, "Climate, Comfort and Natural Ventilation:
A New Adaptive Comfort Standard for ASHRAE
Standard 55", Center of Environmental Design
Research, Center for the Built Environment,
University of California, Berkeley: eScholarship
Repository, 2001, p 2.

Thermal comfort in a building depends upon the individual and the building's ability to provide microclimates, but most public buildings, especially in the US, blast a standard temperature from air conditioners or heaters, regardless of what the weather happens to be on a certain day. Air-conditioned office buildings during the hot Manhattan summers, for example, tend to be set at a constant temperature, which is uncomfortably cold for some body types, but not others. Although they achieve quantifiable environmental standards, these types of buildings are therefore limited in their potential to stimulate a wider sense of temperature.

There are two other common examples of enclosed buildings that eliminate microclimatic differences: the first is the hospital, where windows are often inoperable due to heating and cooling systems, and hospital beds are not always placed in front of window views.[25] The second is the typical Passive House. For some houses to achieve Passive House standard, the north wall will often consist of a thick unbroken thermal mass, with windows facing south for passive solar gain. As a result, Passive Houses sometimes lack light

"It will take mor
technology to ac
degree of chang
decisions are no
reason or ethica

than science and
eve the required
since peoples'
motivated by
mperatives alone."

26 "The Passive House model is satisfactory from the point of view of efficiency metrics. But architecturally, the model has been questioned, if not discredited, because of the enormous investment of insulation and materials at the perimeter in order to prevent any heat from going in or leaking out. That creates an aesthetic challenge because it typically means you're going to have a dreary house with very small windows and not a lot of light." In "Multitasking Infrastructures: A Conversation with Sheila Kennedy and Veit Kugel", The Architectural League of New York's Urban Omnibus, The Culture of Citymaking, 6 March 2013.

27 "The tendency of technological culture to standardize environmental conditions and make the environment entirely predictable is causing a serious sensory impoverishment. Our buildings have lost their opacity and depth, sensory invitation and discovery, mystery and shadow." Juhani Pallasmaa, "Hapticity and Time—Notes on Fragile Architecture", The Architectural Review 5 (1), 2000, p 1.

28 Leatherbarrow, David, "Necessary Qualifications—Design Before, During and After Construction", in Quality out of Control: Standards of Measuring Architecture, Allison Dutoit, Juliet Odgers and Adam Sharr, eds, London and New York: Routledge, 2010, p 118.

29 Ibid., p 118.

and sensual connection with the exterior environment. For example, the book *Passive Houses—Energy Efficient Homes* documents Larch House in Ebbw Vale, Wales, UK, primarily from the exterior point of view since it displays very few photos of the building's interior spaces.[26] For all their good intentions, the problem with such ecological designs is an overemphasis on technology due to ever-increasing amounts of regulations and a tendency to neutralise architectural space.[27]

A number of architectural theorists, including David Leatherbarrow, have criticised the over-abundance of bureaucracy in the building industry. In his essay "Necessary Qualifications—Design Before, During and After Construction", published in the book *Quality out of Control*, Leatherbarrow opposes the building industry's judgement of quality on the basis of an absolute standard intrinsic to the design in question, arguing that when assessing quality in architecture external agencies matter as much as intrinsic worth.[28] Under the rubric of institutions such as LEED, there is a growing pressure for materials to 'perform' in terms of intrinsic R and U values, or, in the case of PV panels, in terms of output of Btu per hour. Leatherbarrow asserts that the materials themselves cannot be qualified until they are put into context over time, and that the artefact should be judged according to its potential to relate to its surroundings:

> Qualities do not exist in themselves, they emerge in specific situations: of formation (natural or artificial), of construction (wet or dry), of use (planned or unforeseen) and of acclimation (illumination, oxidation, saturation, bleaching and staining). I call this interaction and stressed mutualities. This point is difficult because of our dogmatic commitment to 'the things themselves'.[29]

"Thermal comfort in a building depends upon the individual and the building's ability to provide microclimates, but most public buildings (...) blast a standard temperature from air conditioners or heaters, regardless of what the weather happens to be on a certain day."

Overloaded with closed-loop data systems, 'autonomous' ecosystems often dismiss local realities, cultures, environments and traditions, which can come at the price of qualities that enable buildings to connect with and suit their environments.[30]

In parallel with the growth in global technologies, there is an increasing tendency to rely on quantitative measures of quality in architectural culture. In his foreword to *Quality out of Control*, British architect and author Richard Weston advocates a type of quality in architectural design that counters today's technologies: "Cultivating quality [...] could soon, like 'slow food', mean something rather different and yet strangely familiar: durable, locally distinctive goods and buildings flourishing as a counterpoint to the products of advanced global technologies."[31]

For his part, architectural phenomenologist Dalibor Vesely recommends that architects explore culture, symbolism and meaning as an antidote to the constant onslaught of new technologies, planning methods and regulations, which act as a distraction from design. [32] Other designers see technologies such as solar power as a means of underlining the presence of the slow-moving sun, by heightening sensual stimulation and encouraging a gentler pace—when science is absorbed into a humanist point of view, dichotomies between science and design can disappear.

Recent examples of this include suggestions for how to increase thermal awareness or experience while simultaneously fighting climate change. One such way would be to accept thermal adaptation theory into the norms and codes, which is already done in the US through ASHRAE Standard 55, *Thermal Environmental Conditions for Human Occupancy*.[33] Recent revisions include a new adaptive comfort standard (ACS) that allows warmer indoor temperatures for naturally ventilated buildings during summer. Gail Brager, at the Center for Environmental Design Research, University of California, Berkeley, and Richard de Dear, at the Division of Environmental Life Sciences, Macquarie University, Sydney, ask what influences people's thermal sensations, in their critique of the conventional heat-balance model of the body. This outdated model states that thermal sensation is influenced by personal (activity and clothing) and environmental (thermal radiation, temperature, air speed and humidity) factors alone. Instead, Brager and de Dear propose the adaptive model, which they believe to be a complementary theory, according to which factors beyond basic physiology and physics influence people's thermal preferences:

[30] "Instead of having absolute value, these estimations (of quality) are based on the nature and requirements of the situation in which they exist, in which qualification occurs. To be under- or over-qualified means that the element is more or less refined than is appropriate to the situation in which it appears [...] quality is not intrinsic to things." Leatherbarrow, "Necessary Qualifications', p 118.

[31] Weston, Richard, Foreword, *Quality out of Control, Standards of Measuring Architecture*, Alison Dutoit, Juliet Odgers and Adam Sharr, eds, London and New York: Routledge, 2010, p xxi.

[32] Vesely, Dalibor, "On the Relevance of Phenomenology", transcript of a seminar at the University of Houston, Graduate History, Theory and Design programme, 11 December 1984, in cpfourthosis.files.wordpress.com, p 59, accessed 20 November 2015. Vesely argued that phenomenology was the way for architects to achieve authentic experiences of reality, to leave behind the intellectual and abstract world of science, and win back "the tendency to see things the way that people used to see them, as designers or painters. Phenomenology is an attempt to see from the inside—and not to dismiss or criticize from the outside".

[33] "The ACS is based on the analysis of 21,000 sets of raw data compiled from field studies in 160 buildings, both air-conditioned and naturally ventilated, located on four continents in varied climatic zones [...] We also use GIS mapping technology to examine the energy-savings potential of the ACS on a regional scale." G S Brager and R de Dear, "Climate, Comfort and Natural Ventilation: A New Adaptive Comfort Standard for ASHRAE Standard 55", Center of Environmental Design Research, Center for the Built Environment, University of California, Berkeley: eScholarship Repository, 2001, p 1.

34 "Although it was never intended for ASHRAE
   Standard 55 to *require* air-conditioning for buildings,
   practically it is very difficult to meet the standard's
   narrow definition of thermal comfort without such
   mechanical assistance, even in relatively mild
   climatic zones. And the energy costs of providing
   this constant supply of uniformly conditioned air are
   significant, as are the well-known environmental
   consequences associated with this vast energy
   consumption." Ibid, p 2.

35 This insight was offered by Dr Marie-Claude
   Dubois during my doctoral defence entitled
   "Mediating Sunlight—Sensing Solar Cells", at the
   Oslo School of Architecture and Design, in
   November 2016.

Thermal sensations, satisfaction, and acceptability are all influenced by the match between one's expectations about the indoor climate in a particular context, and what actually exists. While the heat balance model is able to account for some degrees of behavioral adaptation (such as changing one's clothing or adjusting local air velocity), it is not able to account for the psychological dimension of adaptation, which may be particularly important in contexts where people's interactions with the environment (i.e., personal thermal control), or diverse thermal experiences, may alter their expectations, and thus their thermal sensation and satisfaction.[34]

Another approach to improving thermal experience and simultaneously minimising carbon footprint would be to accept different performance targets for different rooms, such as by proposing daylight levels that save energy and enrich experience.[35] These examples can inspire new directions for researchers and practitioners involved in the design of buildings and their environmental control systems.

The Gold LEED-certified house discussed in the following chapter follows architectural traditions that are rooted in the concept of *technics* serving *poetics*, as discussed by British architect and academic Dean Hawkes in his book *The Environmental Imagination—Technics and Poetics of the Architectural Environment*. This tradition of exploring the qualitative potential of environmental technologies was born at the end of the nineteenth century, when more precise control and adaptability was established for power and electric light, as well as for heating and ventilation. Subsequently, the possibility arose for re-establishing the relationship between architecture and climate, bringing about the potential for a fundamental change in the nature of architecture itself. The architectural critic Lewis Mumford characterised this transformation as "the quantification of life".

36 Hawkes, Dean, *The Environmental Imagination—Technics and Poetics of the Architectural Environment*, London and New York: Routledge, Taylor and Francis Group, 2008, p 24.

37 Bachelard, Gaston, *The Poetics of Reverie*, Unitarian Universalist Association, US: Beacon Press, 1971, p 6.

38 "We all have some synesthetic linking, and we all experience one type or another of potentially involuntary synesthetic perception. The persistent belief that the different sensorial inputs coming from the world, such as sounds, smells and images would each be perceived by a different sensory organ, such as the ear, the nose or the eyes, and then transmitted to the area of the brain devoted to the specific sensory modality is no longer sustainable. Merleau-Ponty argued that 'synesthetic perception is the rule' [...] Synesthesia is a preconscious synesthetic ability and experience shared by everyone—an experience similar to a stream of sensorial impressions that language organizes in distinct sensory domains, whose division (touch, smell, sight, etc.) and taxonomy have been superseded." Silvia Casini, "Synesthesia, Transformation and Synthesis: Toward a Multi-Sensory Pedagogy of the Image," University of Aberdeen, UK, *The Senses & Society*, vol 12, no 1, Routledge Press, 2017, p 2.

However, in *The Environmental Imagination*, Hawkes makes the point that, unlike Mumford, architects such as John Soane in Britain, Henri Labrouste in France, and Charles Rennie Mackintosh in Scotland, saw the qualitative potential of these developments:

> Soane, Labrouste and Mackintosh have all been represented as forerunners of this change. Their experiments in and implementation of mechanical heating and ventilating of gas and electric light could easily support this interpretation [Mumford's], but in all of their work we see these technological means consistently applied in the service of qualitative ends, *technics* subservient to *poetics*. This is their most important contribution to the history of the architectural environment and is a legacy that can be traced throughout the work of the most significant architects who followed them.[36]

In this chapter I will discuss how environmental technologies in contemporary solar architecture can serve poetic intentions by stimulating perception. The French philosopher Gaston Bachelard explains the relations between sensual perception and poetics thus: "All the senses awaken and fall into harmony in poetic reverie. Poetic reverie listens to this polyphony of the senses, and the poetic consciousness must record it."[37]

Experience of time, temperature, scale and material in architecture. The four themes that I introduced earlier in relation to solar things (time, temperature, scale and material) will also guide the discussion of solar architecture. Again, we must take into account that our experience and perception of the world is multisensorial, and that sensory stimuli become linked in the brain through synaesthesia.[38]

39 "Many researchers are interested in synesthesia because it may reveal something about human consciousness. One of the biggest mysteries in the study of consciousness is what is called the 'binding problem'. No one knows how we bind all of our perceptions together into one complete whole. For example, when you hold a flower, you see the colors, you see its shape, you smell its scent, and you feel its texture. Your brain manages to bind all of these perceptions together into one concept of a flower. Synesthetes might have additional perceptions that add to their concept of a flower. Studying these perceptions may someday help us understand how we perceive our world." Page prepared by Melissa Lee Phillips, https://faculty.washington.edu/chudler/syne.html, accessed 7 November 2020.

40 Leatherbarrow, David, *Building Time—Architecture, Event, and Experience*, London, UK and New York, NY: Bloomsbury Academic, 2020, p. 11.

As before, the manner in which time is perceived in this work follows three main threads of discussion. Firstly, architecture can create the conditions for the occurrence of multisensual stimulation, or synaesthesia, in present time.[39] David Leatherbarrow writes about time in architecture as being compounded into a series of experiences where

> buildings exist not only *in* but *as* time, that as buildings stubbornly hold their ground for days, months, and years they construct and render legible the persisting and predicting dimensions of the present—the sleepless nights in a friend's house, the sidewalk café lunch that passes too quickly, the dreary winters that make the apartment so confining, and so on.[40]

Secondly, architects can heighten awareness of the solar clock by underlining cyclical patterns of sunlight. Thirdly, design can encourage awareness of linear time spans by contrasting new and weathered materials. I name these three different kinds of time "present time", "cyclical time" and "linear time". Paradoxically, the *timeless* element of well-designed architecture is exhibited in the presence of all three types of *time*, because they add to its richness.

"The goal is (...) t
lived aspects o
to the forefront
laws remain in
Hence, while
to measure ligh
the solar projects (...
concepts in a
qualitative

ensure that the
he design come
vhile the physical
he background.
sing technology
and temperature,
him to use scientific
vay that enables
perception."

"Sustainable architecture can connect
time perception with local surroundings
and climate by highlighting topography,
movement of sunlight and wind direction."

In their study *Body, Memory, and Architecture*, Kent Bloomer and Charles Moore point to a lack of presence, not only of the senses but also of their associated modes of perception, especially time, as an ongoing problem in architecture. They were also among the first to write about how mind-body connections are reinforced by multisensory experience:

> What is missing in our dwellings today are the potential transactions between body, imagination and environment; [...] to at least some extent every place can be remembered, partly because it is unique, but partly because it has affected our bodies and generated enough associations to hold it in our personal worlds.[41]

One of the goals of the architecture discussed in this chapter is to generate associations with the changing exterior of the natural environment, especially the passage of the sun. This leads to the next point: that evolving experiences in time provoked by the perception of sunlight bring inhabitants closer to the rhythms of nature. Sustainable architecture can connect time perception with local surroundings and climate by highlighting topography, movement of sunlight and wind direction. Although I have no interest here in reinterpreting Husserl's philosophy, I take inspiration from his use of the term "Nature's time" or what I call "cyclical time". Husserl writes of the necessity of consciousness to link to the living organism of nature through experience, in order for consciousness to be "animate" and synchronised with "Nature's time": "Only by virtue of its experienced relation to the organism does consciousness become a real human or animate consciousness, and only thereby does it acquire a place in the space belonging to Nature and Nature's time."[42]

Solar architecture, then, can provide a material and conceptual framework for the conditions of daily life. By modulating enclosure and exposure, it can concretise the course of the sun, and thereby the passing of the hours of the day and the seasonal cycles. Moreover, slow solar rhythms can be sensed visually and thermally through changing shadow patterns, providing an experience of respite and calm that befits architecture in the age of the internet.

Finally, the passage of time can be represented by contrasting new and weathered architectural materials,[43] which illustrate the dialectics of change and permanence. By engendering "architectural duration",[44] solar architecture can enable inhabitants to see themselves as part of the progression of culture and time, while also, perhaps, triggering a sense of urgency with regards to our relation to the sun and the environment.

[41] Bloomer and Moore, *Body, Memory, and Architecture*, referenced by Pallasmaa, *The Eyes of the Skin*, p 44.

[42] *An Introduction to Husserl's Phenomenology*, Jan Patočka, trans, Erazim Kohák, ed, Chicago and La Salle, IL: Open Court, 1996, pp 139–140, footnote 3: Husserl, Ideas 1.

[43] "Erosion of a surface through weathering exposes newer surfaces of the same material in its depth, at once the erasure of one surface and the revelation of another. Exposure also involves sedimentation and the gathering of residual deposits, the combination of which—subtraction and addition—is the testimony to the time of a building [...]", Mostafavi and Leatherbarrow, *On Weathering*, p 21.

44 "In this sense, architectural duration implies a
   past that is caught up in the present and
   anticipates the future." Ibid, p 64.

45 Olgyay, Aladar, and Victor Olgyay, *Solar Control and
   Shading Devices*, Princeton, NJ: Princeton University
   Press, 1957; Victor Olgyay, *Design with Climate:
   Bioclimatic Approach to Architectural Regionalism*,
   Princeton, NJ: Princeton University Press, 1963.

46 "The Olgyay brothers have been regarded as largely
   responsible for formalizing bioclimatic or passive solar
   design as a discipline within the field of architecture
   during the 1950s." https://lib.asu.edu/design/
   collections/olgyay, accessed 12 December 2020.

47 Addington and Schodek, *Smart Materials and
   Technologies*, pp 51–52.

48 Lovell, *Building Envelopes—An Integrated
   Approach*, New York, NY: Princeton Architectural
   Press, 2010, p 21, note 6.

The senses of time and temperature as they relate to "Nature" and to the design evolutions discussed in this chapter are informed by the work of three important author/architects between the 1950s and 1970s. Three books, *Design with Climate: An Approach to Bioclimatic Regionalism* and *Solar Control and Shading Devices*, both by Hungarian-born brothers Aladar and Viktor Olgyay,[45] and *Thermal Delight in Architecture* by American architect Lisa Heschong, address the relations between time, temperature and climate. While the Olgyays designed and documented architectural screens that were fine-tuned to specific climates and locations,[46] Heschong wrote about the "thermal delight" that results from architecture's mediation of natural elements, especially sunlight and breeze.

More recently, Michelle Addington, Daniel Schodek and Jenny Lovell have reaffirmed the nature of the architectural threshold as a mediator of external natural forces. Rather than adhering to the notion of the insulated wall as an inert boundary separating interior and exterior environments, they recognise that "all change takes place at the boundary".[47] As Jenny Lovell states, "[a] building envelope is an active threshold, 'a zone in which change occurs'. It is responsible for, among other things, modulating between outside and inside conditions to achieve comfort for the human beings within."[48]

49 Heschong, *Thermal Delight*, p 17.

50 'The Heat of the Moment: Lian Chikako
Chang speaks with Michelle Addington',
ArchitectureBoston, vol 16, no 3, fall 2013,
www.architects.org, accessed 8 June 2016.

Like the other architects discussed, Lovell argues that the comfort of the human body should be a starting point when considering the design of integrated building envelopes, and that the complexity of thermal perception merits a more individualised approach than is commonly accepted. Heschong, too, is critical of the application of blanket standards to thermal regulation:

> ASHRAE standards come in to neutralize large office environments after the building has already been designed. [...] There is an underlying assumption that the best thermal environment never needs to be noticed and that once an objectively 'comfortable' thermal environment has been provided, all of our thermal needs will have been met.[49]

Addington proposes that buildings should be heated to a uniform level of 50°F and otherwise maintained through radiant temperature, by positioning the body near a cold area, such as a window, or a radiant heat source, such as an LED television. She asserts that radiant temperature is the most important exchange for the body in a building, and that we should start to think of our bodies in relation to these things:

> There are times when you just want to lay by the window and feel the heat of the sun on your body. There are times when you just want to be in a corner. There are times when you want to feel a fresh breeze. You want to have those opportunities, but so much of our building has been designed to try to control that homogeneous environment. I like to think of it as creating sensual pleasure [...]. Instead of trying to deal with smart glazing, why not invent one tiny panel where the smartness would be in how it directs heat radiation at neck level? That would be discrete and strategic.[50]

51 Mostafavi and Leatherbarrow, *On Weathering*, pp 64, 69–73.

Hence, rather than imposing standard and unchanging temperature and humidity levels for the entire building after it has been designed, the Olgyays, Heschong, Lovell, Addington and Schodek all argue for a subtle and variegated manner of designing for thermal comfort, involving individual user-control and the capacity of the structural skin to mediate the exterior environment in a way that focuses on material energies rather than walls.

In recognition of the complexity and variability of human perception of temperature, among other factors, the home discussed in this chapter counters the tendency of buildings to reduce our experience of heat, light and humidity levels to a narrow range. Instead, it uses tactics based on dynamic interaction with local climate conditions, reinforced by global technologies, to design spaces that circulate air naturally, orienting the structure to the sun and selecting materials with favourable thermal mass or light-dispersing properties to create a series of pleasant microclimates. Such tactics also take inspiration from the passive ecological strategies of Austrian–American architect Richard Neutra, whose shallow pools of water combined with complex louvre systems, such as in his VDL Research House in Silver Lake, Los Angeles, provide shading and capture prevailing breezes as a way of regulating inside temperatures, while also acting as perceptual devices. Recent advances in environmental technologies, such as the ability to finesse levels of oxygen in domestic interiors, or to control spectrums of light to encourage vegetative growth, allow Neutra's microclimates to be modulated further.

An additional way architects can create a sense of connection with the local environment is by choosing materials and fabrication techniques for the building skin that age in response to climate conditions. As David Leatherbarrow explains: "In the time after construction, buildings take on the qualities of the place wherein they are sited, their colors and surface textures being modified by and in turn modifying those of the surrounding landscape".[51] This contrasts with the concept

52 Foster, Hal, *The Art–Architecture Complex*,
London, UK, and New York, NY: Verso, 2011, p 239.

of connectivity in design expressed through the fluidity of curved forms, as in much high-end architecture of the digital age that follows the notion of architectural affect in its formalist definition as discussed in Chapter One. Indeed, such fluidity runs the danger of causing a loss of connection to rootedness of place. Art critic and historian Hal Foster records American sculptor Richard Serra's comment on fluidity as a growing and problematic phenomenon in contemporary art, architecture and design. Serra differentiates between industrial space, which was defined primarily by the frame and grid, and looser, smoother contemporary space, characterised by movement as opposed to framing: "The problem with those fluid spaces is you never feel grounded in them, whereas I'm still interested in grounding the viewer in an experience of place. A lot of those spaces just wash over you."[52]

In line with Serra's thinking, affective architecture is designed to ground the inhabitant in a sense of place. Rather than focusing on either the global or the local at the expense of the other, it attempts to create critical moments in which multiple scales collapse into one another. One way this can be achieved is by using materials that mediate between the surroundings in which a building is rooted and its inhabitants, both in a physical sense and as perceptual devices.

53 Hawkes, *The Environmental Imagination*, p 200.

54 Buell, Lawrence, *The Environmental Imagination: Thoreau, Nature Writing and the Formation of American Culture*, Cambridge, MA and London, UK: The Belknap Press of Harvard University Press, 1995.

For British architect Dean Hawkes, however, the way that materials are assembled in relation to climate and exterior environment has a deeper significance, as the driver of "environmental imagination":

> What is common to these buildings is *environmental imagination*. This is the ability to envision the outcome of the conjunction of form and material, set within the physical facts of the climate and locale, in ways that inform and enhance the purpose and meaning of a building. This lies at the very heart of the architectural project.[53]

Another author who uses the term "environmental imagination" is Lawrence Buell. In his book *The Environmental Imagination: Thoreau, Nature Writing and the Formation of American Culture*,[54] Buell writes of a more "ecocentric" way of being, which includes attentiveness to environmental cycles, devotion to place and a prophetic awareness of ecocatastrophe. The author believes that, along with the environmental crisis, comes a crisis of the imagination, and that there is a need to seek new ways of understanding humanity's relation to nature.

In answer to Buell's call, architects need to take advantage of the potential of emerging environmental technologies to stimulate the imagination. Paradoxically, the flood of inventions spurred by the environmental movement can allow us to avoid the tendency to bypass the designer's agency in favour of science. The growing number of 'green' materials available today, such as solar film-coated glass, allows architects to choose artifices that serve both the technicalities of energy conservation and the poetics of light, and that counter the pervasiveness of predictable environments. Hence different types of new materials, if designed to allow us to engage with the senses, can reach the realm of affective design.

"The discussion o
clarify and identify
design influence
its power to
to intel

affect] aims to
ne ways in which
people and how
do so can be put
ent use."

55 Thrift, "Understanding the Material Practices of
   Glamour", p 291.

56 Ibid, p 290.

57 Picon, *Digital Culture in Architecture*, p 137.

The new and versatile breed of materials being developed today embodies visual, tactile, colour and auditory characteristics. For example, translucent (rather than opaque) PV panels can have a double role, connecting body and environment while collecting energy, perhaps by functioning as skylights that allow views through to the sky. Admittedly, translucent PV panels have lower energy efficiencies than opaque ones, but if perception is our most important architectural parameter after carbon footprint, should they not be considered more often? In Nigel Thrift's mind, the nineteenth-century Parisian shopping arcades beloved of Walter Benjamin depended on materials such as glass and mirrors (similar to solar glass) to create sensual impressions of light and colour: "Materials have been crucial to the generation of alluring spaces. Thus Benjamin's arcades, often thought (mistakenly) to be prototypical capitalist spaces, depended upon the availability of materials like glass, artificial gems, and mirrors to work their magic."[55]

In addition, materials, for Thrift, often belong to historic typologies and therefore express temporal continuity. For example, he believed that Benjamin's Parisian arcades appealed to the sense of memory through incorporating the arch, a form that dates back to the Romans.[56] A similar idea has been promulgated by Antoine Picon, who argues that architecture in the digital age has failed to relate to our deeper sense of memory, as well as to our social condition, by focusing too narrowly on superficial sensuality. He suggests this could be remedied by a new approach to materiality that embodies both individual and social realities:

> How can we reconstruct a dense web of intuitions and analogies that may enable us to rebuild an understanding of how architecture relates to our individual and social destinies? [...] the answer might lie in a new notion of materiality that is emerging under our eyes.[57]

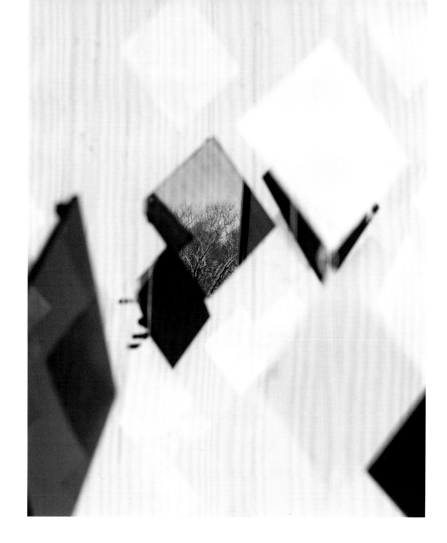

58 Hawkes, *The Environmental Imagination*, p 200.

59 The house was completed in 2019.

60 Partly established by Norwegian architects Knut Knutsen (1903–1969) and Sverre Fehn (1924–2009). As a design, it attempts to work in accordance with Knutsen's particular intentions. He thought that mankind was what mattered. He also felt that "nature is the most valuable and greatest source of inspiration", and that "we must preserve nature by seeking harmony with it and making our buildings subservient to it". Muriel Emmanuel, *Contemporary Architects*, New York, NY: St. Martin's Press, 1980, pp 432–433. http://www. greatbuildings.com/architects/Knut_Knutsen_ Knut_Knutsen.html, accessed 12 December 2020.

61 A classic example of the phenomenon of design not working in synchronicity with nature is the flooding of Mies van der Rohe's iconic Farnsworth House (1945–1951). This masterpiece of International Style was flooded 18 inches (46 cm) above floor level in 2008, after Hurricane Ike.

Architectural materials can therefore embody social realities in various ways— by incorporating local craft traditions, relating to architectural typologies, or addressing cultural norms that evolve out of climate conditions. New technologies applied to architecture require a similar grounding in local craft, climate or tradition, to ensure they remain appropriate to context. By treating PV panels as part of an animated architectural surface rather than as isolated technical systems, solar architecture can therefore embrace mutation and unpredictability, stir the environmental imagination and express cultural continuity.

The house described in this chapter focuses on the behaviour of materials— smart materials as well as more traditional ones—that underline the presence of immaterial natural phenomena and respond to movement and change, as well as to patterns of occupation and perception. Just as importantly, its use of architectural materials and technologies aims to "enhance the purpose and meaning" of architecture,[58] by becoming tools for inventiveness and environmental imagination.

Cocoon House

Cocoon House, in Long Island, New York,[59] stems from the Norwegian architectural tradition of working intimately with nature, which "seek[s] the simple the natural the subdued the immaterial the original and again the natural".[60] Cocoon is thus shaped by aspects of the natural site—the sun and breezes, as well as the surrounding trees and wetland,[61] and explores the theme of contraction and expansion. The house is called Cocoon because its thick, round, opaque walls facing north and west form a cocoon shape.

The design challenge was to serve the view from inside the structure, which was driven by many outside forces, including site constraints and the goal to acquire LEED certification. It also aimed to incorporate environmental technologies such as photovoltaic panels,[62] while at the same time fulfilling complex environmental and perceptual needs. At 16 ft high (4.88 m), the house is split into two parts: a soft opaque shape (the 'cocoon') to the north and west, which retains heat and maintains privacy, and a more transparent, crystalline façade facing south and east, which provides views onto an open landscape and passive heat gain. A legal restriction to build at a 150-ft radius from wetlands, and to keep a 35-ft distance from neighbours towards the north and west, drove the building's L-shaped, 1,730-sq ft (161 sq m) footprint.

The house is located in an environment characterised by a humid continental climate, where it needs to be able to absorb cooling sea breezes during the warm, humid summers, and heat during wet winters. The initial diagram shows the main parameters of the structure and the profiles of its two halves: closed/curved and open/crystalline. Within this overriding schema, the spaces in Cocoon House have been designed to orchestrate events that will awaken perceptions of time, temperature, scale and material, through enhancing sensual experience of the sun and other natural phenomena.

In the open, transparent half of the structure, sunlight filters through translucent skylights, reflects off a water cistern and enters through glass façades, to project onto the interior white ovoid back wall of the house. This thick, egg-shaped wall therefore serves as a screen for the abstract play of light and shadow, and is punctured by just a few small windows. The design of the house aims to stimulate a sense of cyclical time, by directing attention to biorhythms of seasonal and diurnal cycles activated by the sunlight. One of the inspirations for the house was Louis Kahn's Salk Institute in San Diego, California, as observed by David Leatherbarrow:

> If anything is on show in the open space at the courtyard of Kahn's celebrated Salk Institute, it is the interplay of sun, sky and sea, performing as if on a solar stage. Also at play, providing reversals to all that seems stable, are the shadows.[63]

Likewise, Cocoon aims to highlight a range of natural forces at play in the surroundings, such as passing clouds, visible through the translucent skylights, and sea breezes that pass through the sliding doors. The house is also designed to encourage its inhabitants to move throughout the spaces according to changing sunlight patterns and daily rituals, such as dining or reading. In this respect, it relates to American architect and author Ralph Knowles's concept of a "ritual house",[64] as a dwelling that offers choice and variety. For example, the skylights were incorporated into the design to admit direct light into the living area during dark afternoons and evenings, and a sunny spot under the

62 Photovoltaic panels to be installed soon.

63 Leatherbarrow, "Necessary Qualifications", p 112.

64 As outlined in his book *Ritual House—Drawing on Nature's Rhythms for Architecture and Design*, Washington DC: Island Press, 2006, p 28.

65 Neutra, *Nature Near*, p 53.

easternmost south-facing skylight was included to accommodate a comfortable armchair. Additional elements, such as the reflecting pool/cistern and the indoor/outdoor rattan chairs, are similarly intended to stimulate sensual experience and connect the interior with the surrounding landscape. Moving water reflections fill the main spaces and cover almost the entire curved projection screen, like wallpaper, especially on sunny winter mornings when the sun is low, creating the impression of living inside an ocean wave; on the wall of the bedroom hallway, this effect is combined with large moving patches of coloured light. Moving through the home on a sunny day thus involves a cinematic display of natural elements, which connect the interior with the surrounding landscape. These ideas are also in line with Richard Neutra's ideas about architecture promoting behavioural patterns through sensual stimulation:

> In various ways, what he/(she) designs allows people to move and act, but more to the point it also has the effect of impelling them to do so. Far from living or working in a vacuum, the individual is perpetually caught up in his physical and social surroundings, which act upon his organic nature as they impinge upon his senses.[65]

66 Mitsubishi indoor units common in Passive Houses, recommended by Jordan Goldman from Zero Energy Design. The HVAC system consists of four Mitsubishi air-handling units, each of which has a central return. Because heat pumps are air-conditioning systems with a reversing valve that allows one unit to provide both cooling and heating, during the warmer months the heat pump uses a refrigerant to transfer warm air from inside the house to the outdoors; during the winter, the heat pump operates like an air conditioner in reverse, transferring warmth from the outside to the inside, as even in winter the air contains a certain amount of heat. The bathroom heating grills are supplemented with manually operable radiant floor heating for when the temperature is very cold.

In a structure that partakes in the natural landscape, sense of temperature is primarily achieved through passive strategies. The main living area and bedroom corridor has a 65-ft (20-m) long sliding glass wall that opens to catch breezes from the Atlantic Ocean during the warmer months, which, combined with interior shades/curtains, cuts 50 per cent of solar heat gain. In the winter, the glass collects heat from the southern sun, a passive gain that is reinforced by the thermal mass of the super-insulated walls on the northern and western sides. At the same time, the photovoltaic skylights protect the building from excessive solar radiation, as the silicon layer in the a-Si technology absorbs ultraviolet and infrared rays.

Because the structure is well insulated, achieving low U and high R values, the HVAC system, which runs entirely on solar electric power, expends minimal energy. Using ducts that transmit air from the outside, heat pumps deliver cooling and heat in discrete areas through floor grills as a series of microclimates,[66] allowing the body to move between moderate swings in temperature and humidity levels and avoiding the shocks of cold air conditioning in summer, or excessively dry air in winter. As the pumps work at a lower intensity, they also dry the air at a steadier

"Change takes plac
and cognitive ir
encounters is
the bodily sense
the cognitive p
aroused, and per
the perception o
becomes more p

when the sensual
act of affective
ombined: when
are awakened,
vers are likewise
ption, including
energy processes,
verful and precise."

"Buildings take on the qualities of the
place wherein they are sited, their colours
and surface textures being modified
by and in turn modifying those of the
surrounding landscape."

pace and so improve air quality. On cool evenings, an energy-efficient wood-burning fireplace on the north side of the house provides additional heat in the main living area.[67] However, the hearth is designed to create warmth in more than just a literal sense: the northern and western faces of the house are designed to convey softness and opacity,[68] to suggest that this side of the house is 'warm' and enclosed, in contrast to the other sides which are 'cool' and exposed.

Another way the home stimulates sense of temperature is by applying the laws relating to temperature and colour.[69] As the hottest objects appear white (for instance, the filament of an incandescent bulb), and cooler ones red, the coloured translucent skylights above the hallway in the bedroom wing range from almost white (1500 degrees), through yellow and orange to barely red (600 degrees).

Steelmakers and others who heat materials to specific temperature ranges use this temperature/colour relationship. It can be measured precisely by an 'optical pyrometer', which uses the colour of the light emanating from an object to record its temperature, and was applied intuitively in the paintings of the British nineteenth-century Romantic 'painter of light' JMW Turner.[70] According to Dean Hawkes, Turner provided inspiration for the British neo-classical architect John Soane's approach to colour in his London home:

> He was also much influenced by J. M. Turner's experiments in painting [...] Coloured glass in rooflights, yellow to suggest the effect of midday sun and red in the west facing rooflight in conformity with Turner's colour symbolism, where crimson is associated with the evening.[71]

Elsewhere in the house, the cool temperature reinforces the chilly visual aura: "[T]his space was unheated, using the chill of its atmosphere further to signify its distinction from the galleries. This reinforcement of the visual by the thermal might reasonably be said to be characteristic of Soane's imagination."[72]

Inspired by Turner and Soane, the red skylight in Cocoon positioned at the end of the hallway by the main bedroom signals a gradual progression, from bright daylight near the living room to sunset and cooler temperatures in areas associated with rest and relaxation.

In such ways, solar architecture can incite synaesthesia, linking senses of time, temperature and colour so they awaken simultaneously to slower biological sun rhythms. The crimson skylight produces a red triangle of sunlight that moves imperceptibly along the curved white surface of the main bedroom wall, thus

67 Stuv 21 series energy-efficient fireplace, made in Belgium, the only unit on the market approved by the mechanical engineer for LEED certification; this is one of the first applications of this unit in the US.

68 Conceptually, the walls resemble those of "Isabel Berglund's Knit Universe", in which the interior surfaces are knit of soft wool. See "'Isabel Berglund's Knit Universe': Textile Meets Architecture and Landscape in This Witty Knit Piece by Isabel Berglund, a Textile Designer/Artist from The Danish Design School and Central Saint Martins College of Art and Design in London", by David Carlson, Apr 9, 2010, David Report blog, http://davidreport.com/201004/isabel-berglunds-knit-universe/, accessed 12 September 2013.

69 Colour is related to frequency (or wavelength) of light because hot things radiate light (for instance, the filament in an incandescent bulb), and their temperature affects the colour of the light radiated—'red hot' things glow red, 'white hot' things glow white. Temperature is a measure of the internal energy of a material—the hotter a material is, the faster its atoms are moving. See webphysics.iupui.edu, accessed 17 June 2014.

70 en.m.wikipedia.org, accessed 9 September 2014.

71 Hawkes, The Environmental Imagination, pp 7, 11.

72 Ibid, p 11.

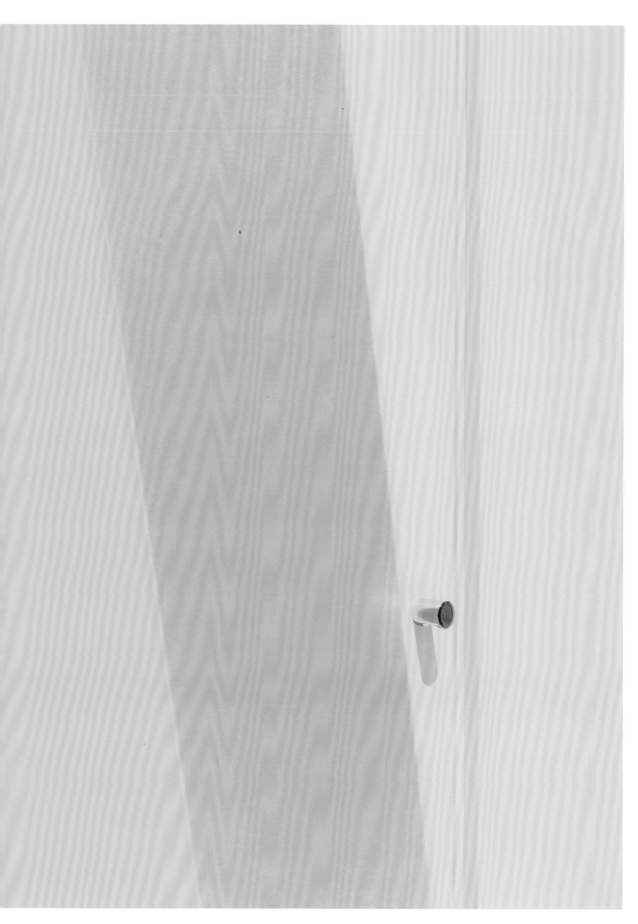

73 Casini, "Synesthesia, Transformation and Synthesis, p 3.

functioning as a type of clock. Because the surface is curved, the shape of the triangle also morphs as it moves, as in an animated film. When the distorted triangle hits the green leaves of the bedroom plant at 7 am in August, it acts as a quiet marker, signalling the hour to make breakfast for the kids before camp; in October, at 10.30 am, the red shape moves to the bed's headboard, promoting a restful feeling on weekend mornings. Meanwhile, in chilly January, the bright yellow triangular illumination projected by the skylight near the kitchen, which moves across the white cabinets, serves as a backdrop to energise cooking brunch. Hence these moving patches of sunlight not only help awaken the sense of time through shifts in colour and temperature, they may also provide a soothing experience for residents and may help filter out extraneous stimuli from our high-tech culture. As Silvia Casini explains:

> Synesthesia may open up possibilities of coping with our existential Western condition of acceleration and excess, which is commonly understood as a sensorial and cognitive over-stimulation alongside constant information flow, all of which are features of today's political, cultural and artistic globalised world.[73]

Other instances of design that stimulate synaesthesia, including sense of temperature, are dispersed elsewhere through the house. For example, the solar chandeliers in the living area become wind chimes when the sea breeze flows freely through the open façade, reinforcing visually and aurally the sensation of

74 Addington and Schodek, *Smart Materials and Technologies*, p 219.

75 Islami, Seyed Yahya, "The Opacity of Glass Rethinking Transparency in Contemporary Architecture," *International Journal of Architecture and Urban Development*, vol. 1, no 2, 2011, p 43.

76 "This early collaboration with engineers was found to be crucial for solar integrated architecture, but was not always easy: architects experienced that engineers 'spoke another language', were often 'too specialized', and 'not willing to compromise on certain issues.'" Kanters, Jouri, Miljana Horvat, and Marie-Claude Dubois, "Tools and Methods Used by Architects for Solar Design", *Energy and Buildings* 68, January 2014, pp 726.

77 It has also been established that timber structures can help play a role in reducing respiratory conditions such as asthma because they give off less pollution than other building materials: "[...] when sourced from sustainably managed forests, wood is the best choice in terms of environmental impact. It uses fewer natural resources and releases less contaminants into the air and water than metal or concrete." https://www.ecohome.net/guides/1010/how-wood-structures-compare-to-steel-and-concrete/, accessed 22 December 2020.

78 The Danby marble originates from quarries in Vermont, less than 500 miles from Long Island.

79 Kronenburg, Robert, *Spirit of the Machine—Technology as an Inspiration in Architectural Design*, UK: Wiley-Academy, 2001, p 62.

a cool breeze on the skin; an armchair is positioned to hear and see rain falling on the glass roof above; an outdoor cooking grill is placed to benefit from the evening sun; and a sofa (Beanie Sofa, Chap Two) situated by the fireside and under a skylight is designed to encourage viewing of the stars or clouds.

The house is therefore conceived not as a sealed, closed-loop system that operates at the singular scale of the building, but as a network of energy-exchanging elements at different scales, in accordance with Addington and Schodek's view that designers should "begin to incorporate an understanding of the simultaneity of scales, behaviors, processes and systems".[74] Hence the translucent, thin-film solar panels are shaped by multiple factors, such as climate and microclimate, building orientation, latitude, longitude, altitude above sea level, distance from the sea, annual irradiation (1,520 kWh/sq m) and average temperature (12.5 degrees Celsius), as well as by specific location. However, in their fluid integration, the panels also act as a connective tissue, collecting energy and functioning as devices that stimulate perception and the imagination. As Persian architectural theorist Seyed Islami explains, "Translucency is about [...] the enchantment of silhouettes, a chiaroscuro of light and shade. Translucency and silhouettes give enough information to leave the imagination free."[75]

To achieve innovation and integration of sustainable technologies can be a challenging process involving a variety of engineering specialisms. In this case, the technical specifications encompassed LEED certification, glass, photovoltaics, electrical, structural and mechanical engineering, and product design, and therefore required extensive collaboration at an early stage in the design process.[76] For example, the HVAC system, which is considerably smaller than normal for a less well-insulated building in the same location, had to be sized by a mechanical engineer, while a geological engineer was needed to create the cistern/reflecting pool that increases luminosity levels, which in turn improve the effectiveness of the nearby solar-powered chandelier and PV panels. However, such technologies can do more than increase efficiency—through its network of ducts in the crawlspace that circulate preheated fresh air from outside, the heat-pump system also serves wellness by improving air quality and promoting healthy lungs.

The parameters that lead to LEED certification also helped guide the selection and distribution of other materials and landscape elements in and around the house, most of which function as perceptual devices. Wood is used throughout the house, including for its structure (curved, laminated timber trusses),[77] flooring (oak) and shingles (cedar), while a variety of stones, including bluestone and Danby white Vermont marble, provide surfacing for the patio and countertops. All are examples of a "primal natural material" obtained from a known source of less than 500 miles distance, and thus contribute to sense of time and place.[78] As Robert Kronenburg writes, "[t]o know what something is made of is to recognize its history. The *primal natural materials* are very few and are intimately related to location—in Western Europe there are perhaps just two: stone and wood".[79]

80 St Benedict Chapel, Sumvitg, Switzerland, 1988.

81 Leatherbarrow, 'Necessary Qualifications', p 115.

82 Ingold, Tim, 'Bringing Things to Life: Creative Entanglements in a World of Materials', Scotland, UK: Department of Anthropology, University of Aberdeen, 2008, p 10.

The cedar shingles that wrap the west-north façades interact with climate and weather conditions, gradually altering the building's skin over time, but in a way that is not always consistent. David Leatherbarrow describes how the colour of the shingles on a chapel designed by Swiss architect Peter Zumthor have been changed selectively by the elements:[80]

> On the north, the shingle has become dark grey in color; on the sunny side, it has retained its reddish-brown hue. These changes do not detract from the building's quality, but in fact enrich it by showing its receptiveness to the characteristics of the place.[81]

In addition to the effects of weathering, the shingles are rooted in the local environment by being steam-bent on site, a technique that originated in Long Island. As an organic building material, they also contribute to insulation and help to keep out the wet and mould that proliferates in the damp climate, by alleviating water vapour. Another factor aimed at improving humidity levels and air quality is the planting scheme, which consists mainly of native beach grass and wisteria growing on the perimeter of the house and the outdoor shower wall; both of these benefit soil and air composition, and signal seasonal cycles. Moreover, because perception of time is closely tied to the olfactory system, the scent of flowers may help awaken memory of place. The surfaces of Cocoon therefore operate as sites of exchange with natural phenomena, reacting continually with surrounding environmental forces to engender a series of affective fields. As Tim Ingold describes:

> Things are alive, as I have noted already, because they *leak*. Life [...] inheres in the very circulations of materials that continually give rise to the forms of things even as they portend their dissolution [...]. It is through their immersion in these circulations [...] that things are brought to life.[82]

"Solar architecture can incite
synaesthesia, linking senses of time,
temperature and colour so they
awaken simultaneously to slower
biological sun rhythms."

The design aim for Cocoon House, then, is to use materials that work with climate forces to influence human experience and perception, including the senses of time, temperature, scale and material. Sense of temperature is aroused by sunlight entering the building and by the warmth of the hearth area sheltered by the thick curved and insulated wall, which contrasts with the open transparent wall and the cooling effect of sea breezes. Sense of scale is heightened by the contraction of the intimate 'cocoon' area covered with cedar shingles, in contrast to the expansive crystalline glass façades that face sky and garden. At the same time, the cedar shingles, which embody local traditions and weather in response to the elements, work in counterpoint with the unchanging coloured PV panels to mark the passage of time, activate cultural memory and contribute to the sense of a sustainable future. On account of this interdependence of design, material and natural forces, Cocoon will be the first private residence in its town to achieve Gold LEED status, and thus carries eco-ethical relevance.

Concluding Thoughts

Each of the four given criteria carries different weight in its contribution to the production of overall affect in the house. For example, the design of Cocoon's living area is influenced mostly by sense of scale, while the glass façade and skylights above the bedroom hallway, though directed at the sky and ocean beyond, are primarily shaped by the senses of time and temperature. At the same time, in nurturing a relationship with the fabric of the existing neighbourhood through materials such as cedar shingles, Cocoon appeals not only to sense of place, but also to cultural memory, and fosters the interrelationships between scales that are required for affective design.

In the history of architecture, there have been two main approaches to incorporating technology: concealing it, and exposing it as a design element. In the first approach, the building's services are invisibly integrated into the fabric, in a process of mystery and deception that, for Nigel Thrift, is fundamental to glamour. To create charm, "[t]he creator must edit out discordant details that could break the spell [...] glamour betokens making what is difficult appear easy".[83] This process of selection, as described by Thrift, is typically expressed in the architecture of Peter Zumthor. In his Kunsthaus Bregenz in Austria,[84] for example, technological services such as ducts and voids are embedded in the structural mass of the walls and floors, in line with the architect's belief that

83 Thrift, "Understanding the Material Practices of
   Glamour", p 299.

84 Completed 1997.

85 Hawkes, *The Environmental Imagination*, p 181.

86 Ibid, p 181.

87 DuBose, Lorissa MacAllister, Khatereh Hadi, and Bonnie Sakallaris, "Exploring the Concept of Healing Spaces", *Health Environments Research & Design Journal*, vol 11(1), 2018, p 49.

88 Addington, Michelle, "Smart Materials and Sustainability", II Strategies–Technology, Werner Lang and Aurora McClain, eds, The University of Texas at Austin School of Architecture, Center for Sustainable Development, 2010, p 7.

"good architecture should receive the human visitor, should enable him to experience it and live in it, but it should not constantly talk at him".[85]

The second approach, where technology is visibly expressed, is exemplified by an architect such as Louis Kahn. In his book on the history of environmental technologies in architectural design, Dean Hawkes cites Reyner Banham's description of the service towers of Louis Kahn's Richard Memorial Laboratories, in Philadelphia, as examples of "exposed power" or "decoration".[86]

In Cocoon, the integration of thin-film photovoltaic panels oscillates between these two strategies—visible exposure of the technology and its invisibility— depending on viewing and sun angles. The house can therefore be said to embody a third approach, which allows technology in architecture to move between the extremes of exposure and camouflage. This more fluid character also enables Cocoon to create an environment that is more likely to promote health. By using technology to engage the senses and heighten awareness of the rhythms of sunlight, particularly when combined with more standard architectural features such as high ceilings, uncluttered spaces and curving walls, it aims to demonstrate that architecture can induce behavioural responses that support mental and physical wellbeing.[87]

Through its application of the chemical, mechanical, electrical and digital sciences, Cocoon attempts to harness the sun's potential more fully, but, above all, to enable the effectiveness of science to merge with the no less significant power of affectivity. The way environmental technologies and strategies combine with materials, site conditions and local craft culture all determine the way light filters inside a structure. If the technological platform can deliver sensual experience, then solar architectural design can spur a host of perceptual revelations. In the words of Michelle Addington: "What matters—and the only thing that matters— is the resulting human perception of that environment."[88]

"The south east
admit sunlight and
throughout the
different ambien
while also contribu
expansion and con
insulated north
preserves the hea
creates a sense

acing skylights

change colour

day to symbolise

temperatures,

ing to the sense of

rasting with the thick,

vestern wall, which

of the hearth and

of contraction."

Chapter Four
CONCLUSIONS

Sensing Solar Cells

1 Merleau-Ponty, quoted by Connolly in "Materialities of Experience", p 182.

Ethical and financial incentives alone cannot motivate people to incorporate environmental strategies and technologies into their everyday lives—they will only do this if they are drawn to them. We therefore need to approach environmental technologies as a series of layered affective zones that have the potential to create allure.

There are two problematic tendencies in sustainable design today. One is the narrow focus on environmental techno-systems; the other, running parallel to it, is the superficial interpretation of the highly debated term *affect*. I have argued that the mainstream understanding of this word leads to an overemphasis on individual sensual stimulation, and is responsible for the exaggerated ornateness of much high-end digitally produced design. This ornateness may speak to the senses, but it often leaves out the important role of design in communicating meaning, including shared ethical imperatives and cultural heritage. Instead of elaboration, designers need to regard their work as a process of distillation that creates the conditions for affective encounters.

Chapter One analysed the problematic contexts in which solar design is currently situated: the need for affective solar design, the debate around affect in the humanities and social sciences, and the agency of the designer in the creation of affect. This chapter also named three issues the designer needs to consider in the creation of affective solar design: the scientific link between sensual and cognitive appeal, which is associated with a Merleau-Pontian mind-body connection; the need to awaken multiple senses—in particular, of time, temperature, scale and material—through synaesthesia; and the imperative for humans to create a "spatiality of situation" in their respective contexts.[1]

The chapter went on to explain how each of the four senses of time, temperature, scale and material gravitates specifically towards one of three concepts: sense of temperature relates to sensual/cognitive appeal, or synaesthesia; sense of scale is associated with the situational; material (primarily, photovoltaic glass) relates to the connection between the lived and the known, or scientific; sense of time originates in the synaesthetic and connects with both the scientific (as sun rhythms are predictable), and the situational (as it relates to the distant solar system).

2 Hansen, Mark, *New Philosophy for New Media*, Cambridge, MA: MIT Press, 2004, p 253.

3 Hensel, Michael, "Performance-Oriented Architecture—Rethinking Architectural Design and the Built Environment," Architectural Design–AD Primers, UK: Wiley & Sons, Ltd, 2013, p 139.

4 DuBose, Jennifer, Lorissa MacAllister, and Khatereh Hadi, "Exploring the Concept of Healing Spaces", The Center for Health Design, Health Environments & Design Journal, 2018, vol II, Sage Publishers, p 48.

However, since each sense contributes a slightly different perception, the more senses are involved in a particular experience, the fuller the experience becomes.

In the case of solar design, the most important sense is temperature, which is experienced in different ways in Cocoon through exploration of the theme of contraction and expansion. Artefacts such as the Sun Calendar wall hanging reflect sunlight patterns in the surrounding environment, amplifying the sun's light and warmth; meanwhile, the south east-facing skylights admit sunlight and change colour throughout the day to symbolise different ambient temperatures, while also contributing to the sense of expansion and contrasting with the thick, insulated north-western wall, which preserves the heat of the hearth and creates a sense of contraction. Materials such as photovoltaic panels also relate to the sense of temperature by acting as mediators for perception through their innate characteristics of liveliness and novelty.

The next theme revolves around the link between situation and scale, reflecting Merleau-Ponty's concept of the spatiality of situation by generating experiences grounded in the human body and context (including sense of temperature), which can then be amplified at scale to produce a potential shift in environmental awareness. Photovoltaic panels connect to the global and molecular scales, but it is up to the designer to link solar works to local and bodily scales.

The most all-encompassing of our four criteria is the sense of time, which is the most deeply linked with affect because affect continually evolves and can only be carried out over time, and thus "*as time*".[2]

The design of Cocoon was born from the many factors that constitute our increasingly complex and vulnerable global world. Among the forces that impinge on it are technology, changing cultural and political values, and unusual weather events, in addition to the growing volume of data produced by our environments, lives and behaviour. The challenge for architects and designers is to accept these conditions and to embrace new technologies without allowing them to become self-enclosed systems unrelated to context, and to find ways of using them that help create mind-body connections charged with affective layers.

As increasing numbers of products and technologies come to market, the more entrepreneurs will be willing to take risks investing in research and design. This is also reflected in the growing number of architectural and design practices versed in the kind of research expected by investors and businesses.[3] The design research carried out in Cocoon was guided by the four fundamental principles outlined above, and the home and all of the individual product designs within it were either scientifically tested, or have been awarded LEED certification. It has also been scientifically proven that quiet environments with access to nature and daylight can support healing and positive thoughts.[4] However, these designs are open to interpretation and are therefore unpredictable in terms of outcomes— without conducting interviews of people who have experienced them directly, we cannot reliably evaluate their affective pull. Moreover, design is about developing

"In the case of solar design, the most important sense is temperature, which is experienced in different ways in Cocoon through exploration of the theme of contraction and expansion."

new modes of thinking in which intuition plays a substantial part. For example, an initial sketch sparked the idea of the walls of Cocoon being half opaque, half transparent, and a hunch initiated the origami model that led to the design of Latitude Lamp. The research paradigm used here is therefore intended primarily to encourage designers to explore the relations that choreograph human experience, including the perceptive process, rather than to think in terms of isolated objects and unchanging laws. The senses intermingle inextricably and design tools 'from without' have only a limited role to play in understanding sensibility 'from within'. Jan Patočka describes this latter type of sensibility as its "living functioning":

How significant [...] can such [objective] results be [...] if we want to understand sensibility [...] in its living functioning? In that case we must bracket such results, not letting ourselves be misled by purely objective outcomes [....] Can we maintain this when we look at the *living* life as lived, analyzing it without the spectacles of a third person, impersonal view?[5]

5 Patočka, Jan, *Body, Community, Language, World*, Erazim Kohák, trans, James Dodd, ed, Chicago and La Salle, Illinois: Open Court, 1998, p 141.

"Sense of temperature is aroused by
sunlight entering the building and by the
warmth of the hearth area sheltered by
the thick curved and insulated wall, which
contrasts with the open transparent wall
and the cooling effect of sea breezes."

Human feeling is continuous and unified, and the individual senses evoke
reactions that create space for other affective fields—synaesthesia, according to
Merleau-Ponty, is a basic characteristic of sensibility. It is also a capacity of which
we are not always fully aware, and it can play a role in helping us access memory
and unconscious experience.[6] Design has the potential to bring that awareness
back, but there can be no purely objective outcomes in this endeavour, only a
continuous effort to focus on potential forms of attachment and attention. As I
have argued above, these questions are particularly relevant today because
designers working in 'green' design struggle to balance design incentives with
environmental technology.

Moreover, architects and designers need to understand solar energy's most
vital tools—such as PV panels—in terms of both energy and affect, and take
advantage of the opportunities for engagement they present. Underlining the
associated senses of time, temperature, scale and material—the four primary
senses that link the sun, solar cells and human perception—offers one way in which
solar technologies can become more deeply engaging and affective, and help
us understand the relations between nature, technology and perception. This
enhanced view of design also needs to be reflected in a transformed approach
to education and training so that it incorporates a wider range of ideas, including
memory and multisensoriality. However, the ultimate test of my study will be its
power to inspire others, to enable designers and visitors to understand solar design
in new and expanded ways, and to send them along richer paths of perception.

6   Casini, Silvia, "Synesthesia, transformation and
    synthesis: toward a multi-sensory pedagogy of
    the image", University of Aberdeen, UK, *The
    Senses & Society*, 2017, vol 12, no 1, Routledge
    Press, p 2.

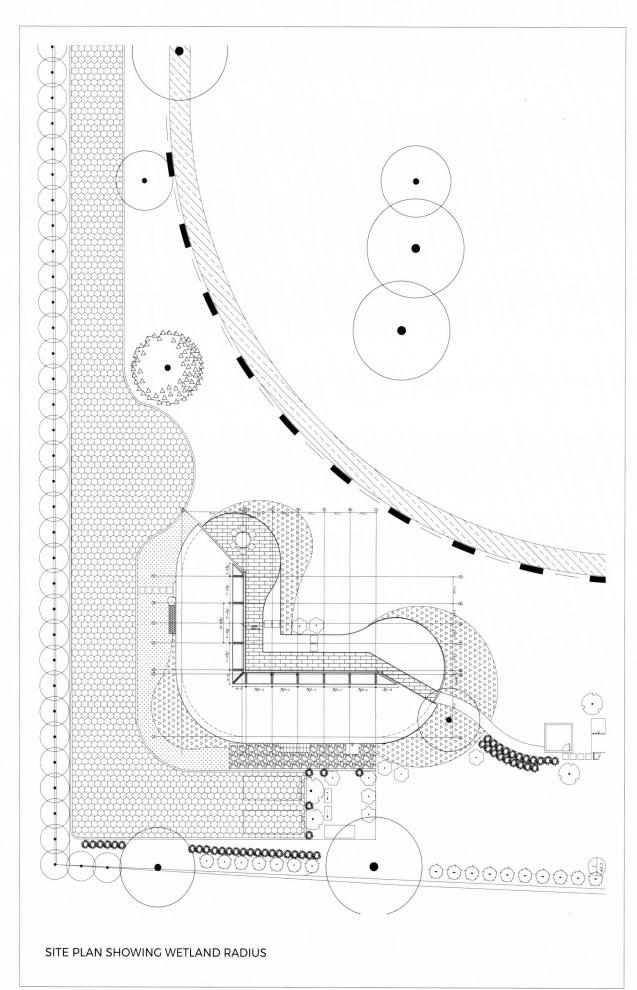

SITE PLAN SHOWING WETLAND RADIUS

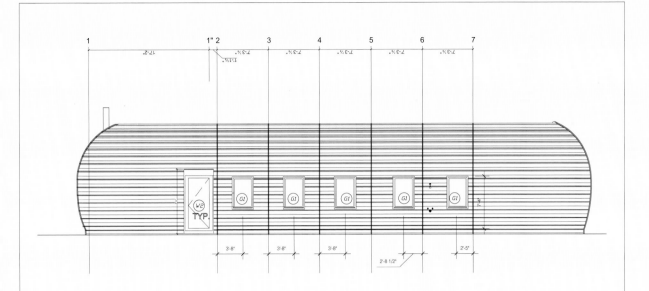

WEST ELEVATION

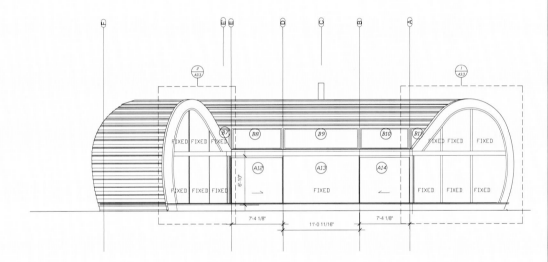

SOUTH ELEVATION

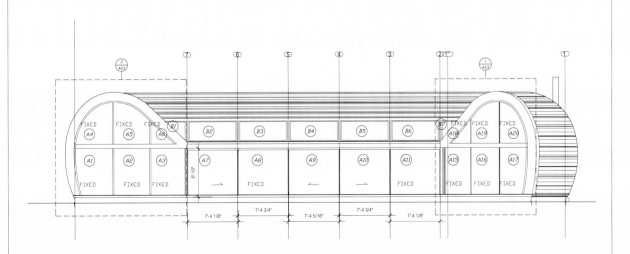

EAST ELEVATION

drawings by Anna Agoston

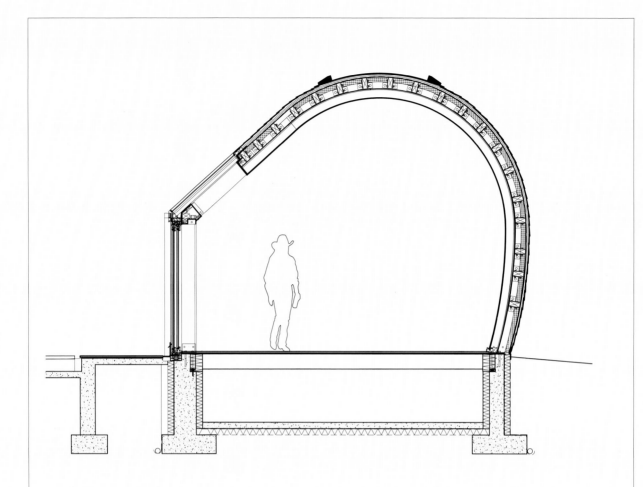

SECTION LIVING AREA

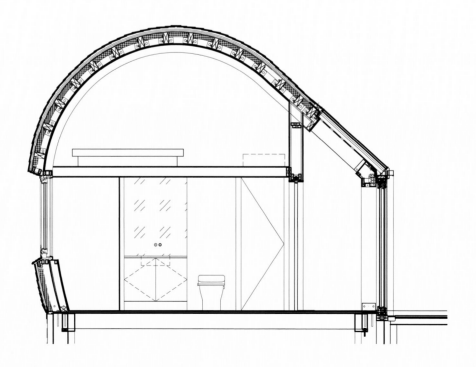

SECTION BATHROOM

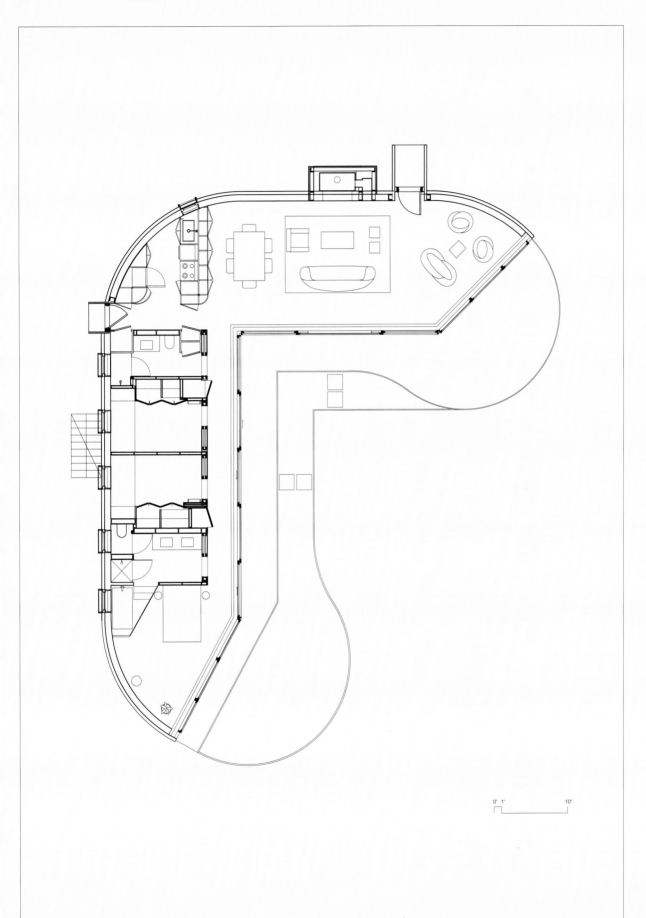

FURNITURE PLAN

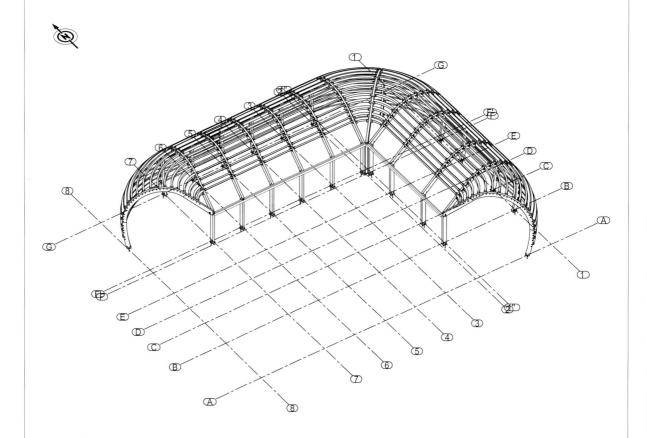

AXONOMETRIC SHOWING TIMBER FRAMING

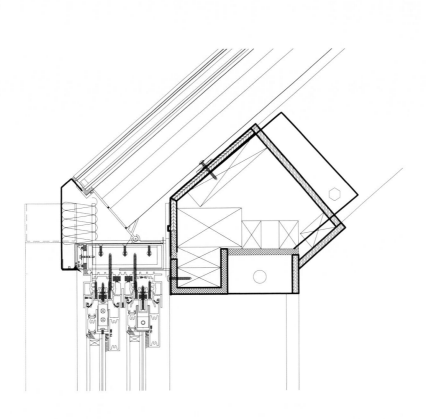

SECTION DETAIL — SLIDING DOORS

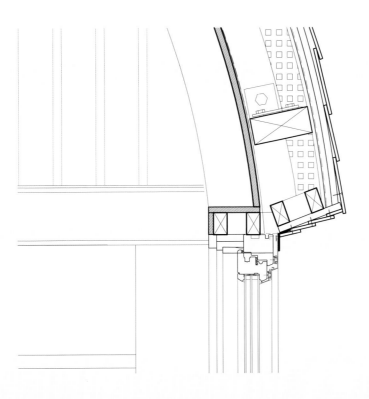

SECTION DETAIL — WINDOW

Bibliography

Michelle Addington and Daniel Schodek, *Smart Materials and Technologies: For the Architecture and Design Professions*, (Oxford, UK, Burlington, MA: Elsevier, 2005)

Sara Ahmed, *Queer Phenomenology: Orientations, Objects, Others*, (Durham, North Carolina: Duke University Press, 2006)

Gaston Bachelard, *La Poétique de L'Espace* (*The Poetics of Space: The Classic Look at How We Experience Intimate Places*, (Paris: Presses Universitaires de France, 1958)

Gaston Bachelard, *La Poétique de la Rêverie*, (Paris: Presses Universitaires de France, 1960), and translated, second edition, The Poetics of Reverie (Unitarian Universalist Association, USA: Beacon Press, 1971)

Gaston Bachelard, *La Psychanalyse du Feu* (1938), (Paris: Éditions Gallimard, 1992), and The Psychoanalysis of Fire, translated by CM Gross (USA: Beacon Press, 1968)

Renaud Barbaras, *The Being of the Phenomenon: Merleau-Ponty's Ontology*, translated by Ted Toadvine and Leonard Lawler (Bloomington and Indianapolis: Indiana University Press, 2004)

Behind the Green Door: Architecture and the Desire for Sustainability, Oslo Architecture Triennale 2013, (Oslo: 2013, curated by Rotor)

Michael Benedikt, *For an Architecture of Reality*, (Santa Fe, NM: Lumen Books, 1992)

Susan Buck-Morse, *The Dialectics of Seeing: Walter Benjamin and the Arcades Project* (Studies in Contemporary German Social Thought), (Boston: MIT Press, 1991)

Lawrence Buell, *The Environmental Imagination: Thoreau, Nature Writing and the Formation of American Culture* (Cambridge, MA and London, UK: The Belknap Press of Harvard University Press, 1995)

Judith Butler, *Senses of the Subject* (New York: Fordham University Press, 2015)

Color, Light, Time in Architecture, Jordi Safont-Tria, Sanford Kwinter and Steven Holl (Zurich, Switzerland: Lars Muller Publishers, 2012)

Diana Coole and Samantha Frost, editors, *New Materialisms: Ontology, Agency, and Politics* (Durham and London: Duke University Press, 2010)

Counter-Experiences: Reading Jean-Luc Marion, edited by Kevin Hart (Indiana: University of Notre Dame Press, 2007)

Jonathan Crary, *Suspensions of Perception: Attention, Spectacle and Modern Culture* (Cambridge, MA: MIT Press, 1999)

Design Innovation for the Built Environment: Research by Design and the Renovation of Practice, edited by Michael U Hensel (London and New York: Routledge, 2012)

Gilles Deleuze and Félix Guattari, *A Thousand Plateaus: Capitalism and Schizophrenia* (Minneapolis, London: University of Minnesota Press, 1987)

Jeannine Fiedler, *Laszlo Moholy-Nagy* (London, UK: Phaidon Press Limited, 2001)

Per Olav Fjeld, *Sverre Fehn: The Pattern of Thoughts* (New York, NY: The Monacelli Press, 2009)

Hal Foster, *The Art-Architecture Complex* (London, New York: Verso, 2011)

Kenneth Frampton, *Kengo Kuma Complete Work*, (London, UK: Thames & Hudson Ltd, 2012)

Maxwell Fry and Jane Drew, *Tropical Architecture for Dry and Humid Climates* (Malabar FL: Robert E. Krieger Publishing Company, Inc., 1964, revised version 1982)

Eugene T Gendlin, *Focusing* (New York: Bantam Books, 2007)

Global Design: Elsewhere Envisioned, Louise Harpman, Mitchell Joachim and Peder Anker (Munich, Prestel Publishing, 2014)

Ron Graziani, *Robert Smithson and the American Landscape* (Cambridge, UK: Cambridge University Press, 2004)

Jeanne Haffner, *The View from Above: The Science of Social Space* (Cambridge, MA: MIT Press, 2013)

Michael Haverkamp, *Synesthetic Design: Handbook for a Multisensory Approach* (Basel, Switzerland: Birkhauser, 2013)

Dean Hawkes, *The Environmental Imagination: Technics and Poetics of the Architectural Environment* (London and New York: Routledge, Taylor and Francis Group, 2008)

Michael Hensel, "Performance-Oriented Architecture: Rethinking Architectural Design and the Built Environment", Architectural Design—AD Primers (UK: Wiley & Sons, Ltd., 2013)

Lisa Heschong, *Thermal Delight in Architecture* (Cambridge, MA: MIT Press, 1979)

Othmar Humm, Peter Toggweiler, *Photovoltaics in Architecture: The Integration of Photovoltaic Cells in Building Envelopes* (Basel, Switzerland: Birkhauser, 1993)

Husserl at the Limits of Phenomenology, edited by Leonard Lawlor with Bettina Bergo, translated by Fred Kersten, revised by Leonard Lawlor (Evanston: Northwestern University, 2002)

Ralph Knowles, *Ritual House: Drawing on Nature's Rhythms for Architecture and Design*, (Washington DC: Island Press, 2006)

Robert Kronenburg, *Spirit of the Machine: Technology as an Inspiration in Architectural Design* (UK: Wiley Academy, 2001)

William C Lam, *Perception and Lighting as Formgivers in Architecture*, edited by Christopher Hugh Ripman (New York, St Louis, San Francisco: McGraw Hill, 1977)

Sylvia Lavin, *Kissing Architecture* (Princeton and Oxford: Princeton University Press, 'Point', series editor Sarah Whiting, 2011)

David Leatherbarrow, *Building Time: Architecture, Event and Experience* (London, UK: Bloomsbury, 2021)

David Leatherbarrow, *Uncommon Ground: Architecture, Technology and Topography*, (London, UK; Cambridge, MA: The MIT Press, 2000)

David Leatherbarrow and Mohsen Mostafavi, *On Weathering: The Life of Buildings in Time*, (London, UK; Cambridge, MA: The MIT Press, 1993)

François Lévy, *BIM: In Small-Scale Sustainable Design* (Hoboken, NJ: John Wiley and Sons, 2012)

Christian Lotz, *From Affectivity to Subjectivity: Husserl's Phenomenology Revisited* (Hampshire and New York: Palgrave Macmillan, 2007)

Ross Lovegrove, *Supernatural: The Work of Ross Lovegrove* (New York, NY: Phaidon, 2004)

Erin Manning and Brian Massumi, *Thought in Act: Passages in the Ecology of Experience* (Minneapolis, London: University of Minnesota Press, 2014)

Jean-Luc Marion, *Being Given: Toward a Phenomenology of Givenness*, translated by Jeffrey L Kosky (Stanford University Press, Stanford, California, 2002)

Jean-Luc Marion, *The Visible and Being Revealed*, translated by Christina M Gschwandtner and others (Fordham University Press, New York, 2008)

Sandro Marpillero, *James Carpenter: Environmental Refractions* (Basel: Birkhauser and released by Princeton Architectural Press, 2006)

Brian Massumi, *Parables for the Virtual: Movement, Affect, Sensation* (Durham and London: Duke University Press, 2002)

Maurice Merleau-Ponty, *La Structure du Comportement*, sixième édition, (Paris: Presses Universitaires de France, 1967)

Maurice Merleau-Ponty, *L'Œil et l'Esprit*, (*Eye and Spirit*), (Paris: Éditions Gallimard, 1964)

Maurice Merleau-Ponty, *Phenomenology of Perception*, translated Colin Smith (London: Routledge, 1962)

Laszlo Moholy-Nagy, *Vision in Motion* (Chicago, IL: P Theobald, ID book, 1947)

Laszlo Moholy-Nagy, *The New Vision: Fundamentals of Bauhaus Design, Painting, Sculpture, and Architecture* (Mineola, NY: Dover Publications, 1938)

Timothy Morton, *Hyperobjects* (Minneapolis, London: University of Minnesota Press, 2013)

Nature Near: Late Essays of Richard Neutra, edited by William Marlin; foreword by Norman Cousins (Santa Barabara, CA: Capra Press, 1989)

New Materialisms: Ontology, Agency, and Politics, edited by Diana Coole and Samantha Frost (Durham and London: Duke University Press, 2010)

Christian Norberg-Schulz, *Genius Loci: Towards a Phenomenology of Architecture* (London: Academy Editions, 1979)

Christian Norberg-Schulz, *Intentions in Architecture* (Cambridge, MA: The MIT Press, 1965)

Olafur Eliasson, edited by Kunsthalle Basel. Exhibition catalogue (Basel: Kunsthalle Basel; Berlin/Muttenz: Schwabe & Co AG, 1997)

Aladar Olgyay and Victor Olgyay, *Solar Control and Shading Devices* (Princeton, NJ: Princeton University Press, 1957)

Victor Olgyay, *Design with Climate: Bioclimatic Approach to Architectural Regionalism* (Princeton, NJ: Princeton University Press, 1963)

Jorge Otero-Pailos, *Architecture's Historical Turn: Phenomenology and the Rise of the Postmodern*, (Minneapolis: University of Minnesota Press, 2010)

Juhani Pallasmaa, *The Eyes of the Skin: Architecture and the Senses* (John Wiley & Sons, Ltd., West Sussex, UK, 2005)

Jan Patočka, *An Introduction to Husserl's Phenomenology*, translated by Erazim Kohák, edited with Introduction by James Dodd (Chicago and La Salle, IL: Open Court, 1996)

Jan Patočka, *Body, Community, Language, World*, translated by Erazim Kohák, edited with an Introduction by James Dodd (Chicago and La Salle, IL: Open Court, 1998)

Antoine Picon, *Digital Culture in Architecture: An Introduction for the Design Professions* (Basel: Birkhauser, 2010)

Antoine Picon, *The Materiality of Architecture* (Minneapolis: University of Minnesota Press, 2021)

Quality out of Control: Standards for Measuring, edited by Allison Dutoit, Juliet Odgers, Adam Sharr (London and New York: Routledge, 2010)

Jennifer L Roberts, *Mirror Travels: Robert Smithson and History* (New Haven and London, Yale University Press, 2004)

Bjørn Normann Sandaker, *On Span and Space: Exploring Structures in Architecture* (London and New York: Routledge, 2008)

Sensing Spaces: Architecture Reimagined (London: Royal Academy Publications, 2014)

SQM—The Quantified Home: Thoughts and Discussions on the Square Meter, edited by Space Caviar (Kortrijk: Lars Muller Publishers, Biennale Interieur, 2014)

Kathleen Stewart, *Ordinary Affects* (Durham & London: Duke University Press, 2007)

The Affect Theory Reader, edited by Melissa Gregg and Gregory J Seigworth (Durham and London: Duke University Press, 2010)

The Landscape Urbanism Reader, edited by Charles Waldheim (New York, NY, Princeton Architectural Press, 2006)

The Perception of the Environment: Essays on Livelihood, Dwelling and Skill (London and New York: Routledge, 2000)

The Routledge Companion to Research in the Arts, edited by Michael Biggs and Henrik Karlsson (London and New York: Routledge Taylor and Francis Group, 2011)

James Turrell, Fundacion NMAC (Milano: Edizioni Charta, 2009)

Vitamin Green, edited by Joshua Bolchover, Johanna Agerman Ross, FXFOWLE (London: Phaidon Press Limited, 2012)

Biographical Note

Dr Nina Edwards Anker is an internationally recognised architectural design professional, founder and principal of nea studio, a firm in New York City that focuses on sustainable architecture and design. Nina is a design director at Terreform One, a non-profit architecture and urban think tank, and a founding member of Newlab, a multidisciplinary technology centre, also both in New York City. She holds a PhD from the Oslo School of Architecture and Design and an MArch from Harvard Graduate School of Design, and also teaches environmental design at various universities. Her Cocoon House won the 2020 AIA Long Island Award for Innovation in Sustainability and the Domus 2019 Best Houses Award.

Acknowledgements

This book is made possible by a grant from the Oslo School of Architecture and Design (AHO). Thank you Professor Bjørn Sandaker at AHO, as well as Professor Mitchell Joachim of New York University for your work guidance.

I thank Vivian Kuan and Mitchell Joachim for inviting me to participate in design reviews and studio projects over the past few years, with the research fellows at Terreform ONE, as well as Lisa Richardson, who continually inspire me to think critically and innovatively. Special thanks to Anna Agoston, Hedevig Anker, Carina Balg, Bothild Bendiksen, George Berenz, Charlotte Cousins, Einar Dahle, Marie-Claude Dubois, Karl Otto Ellefsen, Melanie Fessel, Deziree Guedez, Lise Hansen, Louise Harpman, Tjasa Kalmbach, Janike Kampevold Larsen, Alice Labadini, David Leatherbarrow, Joe Licciardi, Pavlina Lucas, Sia Mahdavi, Thomas McQuillan, Michael Miller, Mia Mochizuki, Joe Moltz, Andrew Morrison, Angelika Morrison, Kari Nøst Bergem, Sabrina Pagani, Antoine Picon, Ninni Rautiainen, Maxime Richard, Børre Skodvin, Nader Tehrani, Sofie Vertongen, Pilar Viladas, Raphael Walther, Marek Walczak, Magne Wiggen, Raphael Wloski and my Greeven cousins Andrea, Cristina, Caroline and Amely.

This book is dependent on the team at Artifice Press, the suggestions of Anna Danby, Publishing Director, the project management of Daphne Fordham-Smith and the graphic design of Rachel Pfleger. Davina Thackara meticulously reviewed and edited the text.

Deepest gratitude to Peder Anker for continuous support, Michael Edwards for brilliant electrical engineering and to Philip Edwards and family—Ali, Veronica, Zinnia and Patrick—for sharing this property with us.

This book is dedicated to my boys, Lukas and Theo—may you fly from this home like butterflies from a cocoon, with your deepest colors showing.

Credits

COCOON HOUSE

Project Leader
Nina Edwards Anker

Architectural Design Team
Anna Agoston
Raphael Walther

Building Contractors
Licciardi Builders
Lynbrook Glass
Unalam
Lance Nill Inc

Advisors
Mitchell Joachim
Bjørn Normannn Sandaker

Structural Engineer
Alexey Nefedov
Will Laufs, LED

**LEED Consultant/
Mechanical Engineer**
Jordan Goldman,
Zero Energy Design

LEED Verification
Karla Donnelly,
Steve Winters Associates

Photography
Caylon Hackwith
Costas Picadas
Naoko Maeda

ALGAE LAMPS

Credits
Joy Peng
Deziree Guedez
Nicole Bach
Shahira Hammad
Leo Cheng
Yen-Chieh Chiu (Andrew)

KNOTTY SET

Fabricator
Onyx Furniture

CANTILEVER TABLE

Fabricator
Milgo Bufkin

CRYSTALLISED TABLE

Fabricator
Ferra Design

CRYSTALLISED CHAIR

Fabricator
Ferra Design

VANITY TABLE

Fabricator
Synthetix

BIRD CHAIR

Fabricator
Milgo Bufkin

LATITUDE LIGHT

Drafting and Assembly
Raphael Walther
Shahira Hammad

Production Manager
Yen-Chieh Chiu (Andrew)

Electrical Engineers
Dave Young,
Young Circuits Designs
Michael Edwards, avioWorks

SUN CALENDAR

Drafting, Assembly
Carlos Cardenas

Electrical Engineer
Michael Edwards, avioWorks/
Eric Forman, Forman Studio

SOLAR CHANDELIER

Drafting, Assembly
Shahira Hammad
Federica Dattilo

Electrical Engineer
Michael Edwards, avioWorks

SOLAR LOUNGER

Credits
Raphael Walther

Electrical Engineering
Michael Edwards, avioWorks

Mechanical Engineer
Harris Enotiades

© 2021 Artifice Press Limited, the architect and the authors.

Artifice Press Limited
298 Regents Park Road
London N3 2SZ
United Kingdom

+44 (0)20 8371 4047
office@artificeonline.com
www.artificeonline.com

Designed by Rachel Pfleger
Cover design by Jochen Viegener
Edited by Davina Thackara

All opinions expressed within this publication are those of the authors and not
necessarily of the publisher.

British Library in Cataloguing Data. A CIP record for this book is available from
the British Library.

ISBN 978-1-911339-39-7

Printed in the United Kingdom by Kingsbury Press Ltd on Revive Silk 170gsm.
This paper has been independently certified according to the standards of the
Forest Stewardship Council® (FSC)®.